THE TEACHERS & WRITERS
Handbook
of
Poetic Forms

THE TEACHERS & WRITERS

Handbook

of

Poetic Forms

Edited by Ron Padgett

Teachers & Writers Collaborative
New York

The Teachers & Writers Handbook of Poetic Forms

Teachers & Writers Collaborative
5 Union Square West
New York, N.Y. 10003

Library of Congress Cataloging-in-Publication Data
The Teachers & writers handbook of poetic forms.

Summary: A reference guide to various forms of poetry with entries arranged in alphabetical order. Each entry defines the form and gives its history, examples, and suggestions for usage.
 1. Poetics. 2. Versification. 3. Literary form.
[1. Poetics 2. Versification 3. Literary form.]
I. Padgett, Ron. II. Teachers & Writers Collaborative.
III. Title: Teachers and writers handbook of poetic forms.
PN1042.T43 1987   808.1   87-6455
ISBN 0-915924-24-2
ISBN 0-915924-23-4 (pbk.)

Printed by Philmark Lithographics, New York, N.Y.
Fifth printing

Acknowledgments

Teachers & Writers Collaborative receives funds from the New York State Council on the Arts and the National Endowment for the Arts.

T&W programs and publications are also made possible by funding from American Broadcasting Companies, Inc., American Stock Exchange, Columbia Committee for Community Service, Consolidated Edison Company, Fund for Poetry, General Electric Foundation, Herman Goldman Foundation, KIDS Fund, Long Island Community Foundation, Mobil Foundation, Inc., Morgan Guaranty Trust Company, Morgan Stanley, New York Telephone, The New York Times Company Foundation, Henry Nias Foundation, Pisces Foundation, Primerica Foundation, Helena Rubinstein Foundation, and The Scherman Foundation.

T&W extends special gratitude to Mr. Bingham's Trust for Charity for its extraordinary commitment to fostering writing and creative thinking skills in children.

The editor wishes to thank Gary Lenhart, Bernadette Mayer, Chris Edgar, and Nancy Shapiro for their editorial help.

Gratitude is also due to the following publishers and writers who permitted T&W to use selections from their work:

Event poem from *Assemblages, Environments, Happenings* by Allan Kaprow, published by Harry N. Abrams, Inc. All rights reserved.

"Tooting My Horn on Duty" excerpted from *So Going Around Cities: New and Selected Poems 1958-1979,* copyright © 1980, 1987 by Ted Berrigan and The Estate of Ted Berrigan, reprinted here by permission of Blue Wind Press, P.O. Box 7175, Berkeley, CA 94707.

"Ode to the Watermelon" reprinted from *Neruda and Vallejo: Selected Poems,* Beacon Press, 1971. Copyright © 1970 by Robert Bly, reprinted by his permission.

"The Painter" from *Some Trees* and "To a Waterfowl" from *Locus Solus 2* (1961) reprinted by permission of Georges Borchardt, Inc. and John Ashbery. Copyright © 1956 by John Ashbery (*Some Trees*); copyright © 1961 by John Ashbery ("To a Waterfowl").

Contents

Poetic Forms
Abstract Poem 1 • Acrostic 5 • Allegory 7 • Alliteration 9 •
Alphabet Poem 12 • Assonance 15 • Ballad 17 • Ballade 21 •
Blank Verse 24 • Blues Poem 28 • Bouts Rimés 31 •
Calligram 33 • Canto 37 • Canzone 39 • Cento 41 • Chant
44 • Cinquain 48 • Collaboration 50 • Concrete Poem 52 •
Couplet 57 • Eclogue 60 • Elegy 62 • Epic 65 • Epigram 67
• Epistle 70 • Epitaph 72 • Epithalamium 74 • Event Poem
76 • Foot 79 • Found Poem 82 • Free Verse 85 • Ghazal 87
• Haiku 89 • Imitation 92 • Insult Poem 95 • Light Verse 97
• Limerick 98 • Line 100 • List Poem 104 • Lune 107 •
Lyric 110 • Macaronic Verse 113 • Madrigal 116 • Metaphor
118 • Nonsense Verse 122 • Occasional Poem 124 • Ode 125
• Ottava Rima 131 • Pantoum 133 • Parody 136 • Pastoral
Poem 140 • Performance Poem 142 • Projective Verse 148 •
Prose Poem 151 • Quatrain 153 • Rap 155 • Renga 159 •
Rhyme 163 • Rhythm 165 • Ritual Poem 167 • Rondeau
171 • Satire 174 • Senryu 179 • Sestina 181 • Skeltonic Verse
186 • Sonnet 189 • Spoonerism 192 • Stanza 194 • Syllabic
Verse 186 • Tanka 198 • Tercet 200 • Terza Rima 203 •
Triolet 205 • Villanelle 208 • Word Play 212

Table of Figures

Preface

We began to compile *The Handbook of Poetic Forms* for secondary school students and their teachers, but as we went along we realized it could be useful for anyone interested in learning about poetic forms.

The *Handbook* entries were prepared by creative writers who have taught poetry writing to young people, mostly in the Teachers & Writers Collaborative program. These writers know how important it is to present their material in a clear, friendly, and straightforward manner, without getting mired in the technicalities that interest specialists more than young people. Part of the very reason for this book — essentially a poetics reference book for young people and novice writers — is that nothing like it exists.

The *Handbook* contains seventy-four entries by nineteen writers. There was much discussion as to which forms to include and which not. We don't claim to have made the perfect selection; we doubt that there is such a thing. Our ultimate criterion was whether or not a young person might enjoy learning about a form by using it. And so, we include some forms rarely (if ever) listed in poetics handbooks, such as the lune, and we omit some traditional forms, such as the aubade. We've thrown in a couple of old forms that have fallen into disuse, with the hope that they might be re-explored. Our intention was not to compile an encyclopedia, but rather a handbook that people would enjoy using both as a reference book and as a guide for writing.

We have also been flexible in our notion of what "form" is. In fact, we include entries that are not forms at all. In some cases they are *genres* (types) of writing, such as satire; in others they are *methods* of writing, such as collaboration (two or more people writing together). We include these other entries because we feel they help create a better sense of what it is like to use the various forms. And, as you will see, some of the forms don't have strict rules.

We're reminded of the poet who once received a letter congratulating him on his mastery of particular form, as described in a poetics handbook. The poet had neither heard of the form nor could he find other examples of poems in that form. He concluded that the handbook editor had read his poem, "seen" a form in it, given the form a name, and then used the poem as an *example* of that form! It's nice to learn that not only do you fit into a literary tradition, you *are* the tradition.

The entries in this handbook are arranged in alphabetical order. Each entry defines the form, summarizes its origins and history, provides examples (where practical), and gives advice on how to write in that form.

Directly below each entry heading is a phonetic spelling of the heading. For instance,

Pantoum
("pan-TOOM")

The syllable in capital letters is the one that gets accented. Keep in mind that although the phonetic spelling is fairly accurate, it is highly simplified and in some cases not so precise as it would be in a good dictionary.

•

Many entries are cross-referenced whenever they have enough in common to make it worthwhile to think about them in relation to each other. And so, for instance, at the end of the entry for Couplet, it says, "See also: FOOT, LINE, EPIGRAM, and SONNET."

Some forms and techniques are discussed under other headings. For a list of these, see Appendix A. For further reading on the various forms, consult the Bibliography.

Also included (Appendix B) is a list of authors mentioned in the *Handbook*, giving their dates and a brief identification.

There are several good reference books on poetics (see Bibliography). The best is the *Princeton Encyclopedia of Poetry and Poetics,* edited by Alex Preminger. It is an outstanding piece of work, but its detail and high level of scholarship make it unsuitable for the average young person or novice writer.

The editor would like to thank the writers who helped prepare the *Handbook*: Reed Bye (ballad, Skeltonic verse, tercet), Jack Collom (lune, parody), Harry Greenberg (abstract poem, alphabet poem), Penny Harter (renga), Geof Hewitt (alliteration, assonance, found poem, limerick, rhyme, rhythm, spoonerism, syllabic verse, word play), William J. Higginson (cinquain, haiku, tanka, renga, senryu), Roland Legiardi-Laura (rap, satire), Gary Lenhart (epistle, line, lyric poem, stanza), Geri Lipschultz (ode), Mary Logue (elegy, ghazal, villanelle), Bernadette Mayer (allegory, canzone, collaboration, epic, epigram, macaronic verse, pastoral poem, quatrain, sonnet, terza rima), Suzie Mee (event poem, ritual poem), Susan Mernit (chant, insult poem), Richard Perry (blues poem), Mark Statman (ballade, canto, concrete poem, eclogue, madrigal, projective verse), Anne Waldman (rondeau, sestina, performance poem, triolet, villanelle), Jeff Wright (couplet, list poem), Bill Zavatsky (blank verse, foot, free verse, metaphor), and Alan Ziegler (prose poem, occasional poem). The editor prepared the entries for the acrostic, bouts-rimés, cento, calligram, epitaph, epithalamium, imitation, light verse, nonsense verse, ottava rima, and pantoum. All poems quoted without an author's or translator's name under them are by the entry's author.

If you have any suggestions for future editions of the *Handbook*, please feel free to send them to Teachers & Writers Collaborative.

Hail Muse! et cetera.
— *Byron*

Abstract Poem

Dame Edith Sitwell (1887-1964) used the term *abstract* to describe the poems in her book *Façade*. These poems were experiments in "patterns in sound." They mirrored in language what abstract painters achieve visually, with colors, shapes, and designs that represent no physical objects: it is the paint itself that becomes important. Dame Edith used sound the same way, as in these two excerpts:

> Nobody comes to give him his rum but the
> Rim of the sky hippopotamus-glum
>
> *
>
> Said King Pompey the emperor's ape,
> Shuddering black in his temporal cape
> Of dust, 'The dust is everything —
> The heart to love and the voice to sing,
> Indianapolis
> And the Acropolis,
> Also the hairy sky that we
> Take for a coverlet comfortably.'

In this type of work, the *meaning* of the words becomes secondary to their sound.

Abstract poetry never became a literary movement. But many poets have written poems that might be classified as abstract poems. The nonsense poetry of Lewis Carroll is abstract, as in his "Jabberwocky":

> 'Twas brillig, and the slithy toves
>   Did gyre and gimble in the wabe;
>   All mimsy were the borogoves,
>   And the mome raths outgrabe.

1

Some of Gertrude Stein's writings have the feel of abstract prose poems:

> A little lunch is a break in skate a little lunch so slimy, a west end of a board line is that which shows a little beneath so that necessity is a silk under wear. That is best wet. It is so natural, and why is there flake, there is flake to explain exhaust.
> —*From* Tender Buttons

So does the prose of James Joyce's *Finnegans Wake.*

The hailstorm of imagery common to much surrealist poetry tends to make that poetry abstract, as in these lines from Bill Knott's *Nights of Naomi:*

> Prefrontal lightning bolt too lazy to chew the sphinx's
>   loudest eyelash
> Not even if it shushes you with a mast of sneers
> Down which grateful bankvault-doors scamper
> Because of a doublejointedness that glows in the dark
> Like a soliloquy of walnuts
> Numbed by beaks of headless measuringtape
> So the lubriciousness can tower in peace
> Like a buzzsaw trapped in a perfumery of shrugs
> Lemon
> Or lime
> Only a maze can remember your hair of buttered blowguns

These lines are abstract because of their dense and bizarre images, not because of their sound.

Here are other examples of abstract poems.

> Clothing, sing-worms, and fail! my joyous gasoline
> And caney stars, O spillwort!" Ape. Ate. Ben-
> Seeds was late, oop! he went to high school
> In a, ork! yes a blimp, oh married to the knees
> Of not having, Indian as sharks, the reefed money
> To order O doughtnut coconuts there, weird
> As mated, alcohol, the "ginger," a synco-
> Pation, "Anagrams! fish! pools! babe! hospital
> Of the careful linguist-itch-hand-fields-youthful-
> Kentucky!" Evenings, places, a, it is a. . . .
> —*From* When the Sun Tries to Go On *by Kenneth Koch*

Notice in the following two poems by Clark Coolidge that the further that words are removed from sentences and meaning, the more we focus on their sound:

ounce code orange
a
     the
           ohm
trilobite trilobite

*

of   about

since   dot

There are any number of ways to learn about writing abstract poems. One is to pick a word and say it aloud over and over until it loses its meaning. That'll get your mind focused on sound. Then just write, as quickly as you can, whatever words come to you because of their sounds.

Another method involves taking a poem by you or someone else and changing most of the words. Count the number of nouns in the poem, the number of adjectives, and the number of verbs. Then make a list of an equal number of new nouns, adjectives, and verbs — all of which you choose just because you like their sounds (not their meanings. Also, don't worry about their not making sense as a group.) Then use your lists to replace the corresponding words in the poem. You'll find that some will work better than others, and you'll probably want to adjust the verbs a little.

A third way to make abstract poems is to take a poem and remove (perhaps with white-out) enough of its words so that the remaining words make no sense, but sound good together.

"Sound poetry" is abstract poetry written specifically to be read aloud. It uses language closer to Clark Coolidge's than Edith Sitwell's; that is, the language is "broken up." Sound poetry, which came in part from the Dada poetry created around 1920, has enjoyed a certain popularity in Europe since the 1940s.

See also: NONSENSE VERSE.

Acrostic
("uh-CROSS-tic")

The word *acrostic* comes from the Greek *acros* (outermost) and *stichos* (line of poetry). As a literary form, the basic acrostic is a poem in which the first letters of the lines, read downwards, form a word, phrase, or sentence. For example, in the following short acrostic, the vertical word is "our":

> Open your mind to the
> Universe, and
> Run back home and get your lunch.
>   *—Juan Lugo, seventh grade*

Some acrostics have the vertical word at the end of the lines, or in the middle. The *double acrostic* has two such vertical arrangements (either first and middle letters or first and last letters), the *triple acrostic* has all three (first letters, middle, and last). Here is what might be called a run-on double acrostic, with the last letter of each line capitalized only to make the example clearer:

> Many times I
> Yelled across the cosmoS
> Not knowing to whoM
> And/or what everlasting top bananA
> Men had sought in faR
> EternitY.

The acrostic originated in ancient times and was used in Greek, Hebrew, and Latin literature. Some of the Biblical Psalms (in Hebrew) are acrostics. Authors who used acrostics include Plautus, Boccaccio, Chaucer, Ben Jonson, and Edgar Allan Poe, whose poem "A Valentine" uses the first letter of his beloved's name as the first letter of the first line, the second letter of her name as the second letter of the second line, and so on down, so that her name formed a diagonal from the top left to the bottom right of the poem.

Some ancient writers felt the acrostic had mystical power, but some later writers regarded the acrostic as an empty and trivial game. But any poetic form is trivialized by poor use, and the emptiness is the author's fault, not the form's. Besides, there is playfulness in all poetic forms.

Acrostics are easy to write. First, you write vertically the word or phrase, then go back and fill out the lines, using as many words as you like. Try it with your own name. The acrostic is good for developing mental and verbal agility, especially when written at top speed. It is interesting to turn a word or phrase on its side and see what spills out.

See also: WORD PLAY.

Allegory
("AL-leh-gory")

The word *allegory* comes from two Greek words: *allos* meaning "other" and *agoreuein* meaning "to speak."

An allegory is a story whose characters, things, and happenings have another meaning. Allegories are written to explain ideas about good and evil, or about moral or religious principles. What makes a piece of writing an allegory is that the characters actually *become* what they stand for, and can have names like Ms. Love, Mr. Peace, or Mrs. Evil.

Allegories have been written in the forms of both poetry and fiction. Aesop's fables and parts of the Bible are allegories. Other famous allegories are Dante's *Divine Comedy*, Spenser's *Faerie Queene*, and Bunyan's *Pilgrim's Progress*.

Pilgrim's Progress is the most traditional allegory written in English. Its author, John Bunyan, who lived in England in the 17th century, was considered to be poorly educated compared to the other writers of his time and was imprisoned for being a self-styled religious preacher. During his imprisonment he began to write *Pilgrim's Progress*. The book is in the form of a dream. The main character, Christian, travels from a small town to a big city. On his way from the City of Destruction to the Celestial City, he passes through places called the Slough of Despond, the Delectable Mountains, By-path Meadow, Doubting Castle, the Valley of Humiliation, and Vanity Fair. He encounters many friends and foes, including people named Faithful, Hopeful, Mr. Worldly Wiseman, Mr. Great-heart, Lady Feigning, Madam Bubble, Talkative, Mr. Fearing, Apollyon the Destroyer, Mr. Valiant-for-truth, and Mr. Cruelty.

Bunyan's book begins this way:

> As I walked through the wilderness of this world, I lighted on a certain place where was a Den, and I laid me down in that place to sleep: and as I slept I dreamed a dream. I dreamed, and behold, I saw a man

clothed with rags, standing in a certain place, with his face from his own house, a book in his hand, and a great burden upon his back. I looked, and saw him open the book and read therein; and as he read, he wept and trembled; and not being able longer to contain, he brake out with a lamentable cry, saying, "What shall I do?"

A good method of beginning to write an allegory is to make the whole story be a dream, as Bunyan did. Dreams *are* allegories because in dreams one thing often means something else even though we might not understand or believe it: dreams of spiders or peanuts may mean good fortune. Also, in dreams one person may stand for or symbolize another person or quality: a dream of someone who reminds you of your father may be a dream of your real father, or, if you happen to know two Maria's, you may dream about one and really mean the other. In dreams people can also *become* ideas, for instance, someone could stand for or symbolize Fear.

Famous examples of writing that is not strictly allegorical but has allegorical tendencies include: Goethe's *Faust*, which is about selling your soul to the devil, Ibsen's *Peer Gynt,* Hawthorne's novel *The Scarlet Letter* and his short story "The Bosom Serpent," Melville's *Moby Dick*, in which the white whale represents both good and evil, and James Joyce's *Ulysses*, which is based on Homer's *Odyssey.*

Allegory is much like metaphor — one person or thing *is* another, and not just *like* another (which would be a simile). An allegory could be called an extended metaphor — extended sometimes for 300 pages or more!

Structures and forms in literature are always a result of the way people think. People often think of something that simultaneously reminds them of other things. Allegories are a reflection of this phenomenon.

See also: METAPHOR.

Alliteration
("al-lit-er-A-shun")

The word *alliteration* comes from the Latin, meaning "letters next to each other." Alliteration is the repetition of stressed, initial sounds of words. These repeated sounds are usually made by consonants. Alliterative *effect* occurs when the repeated sound is neither stressed nor initial. Here's an example of both alliteration and alliterative effect:

> It was her voice that made
> The sky acutest at its vanishing.
> She measured to the hour its solitude.
> She was the single artificer of the world
> In which she sang. And when she sang, the sea,
> Whatever self it had, became the self
> That was her song, for she was the maker. Then we,
> As we beheld her striding there alone,
> Knew that there never was a world for her
> Except the one she sang and, singing, made.
> —*From Wallace Stevens' "The Idea of Order at Key West"*

Alliteration is like rhyme, but where rhyme's repeated sound consists of at least one syllable, alliteration requires only the repetition of a *unit* of sound, the sound of a single letter.

Sometimes different letters sound identical. For example:

> A quick cat never lets you know its mind,
> Keeps its cautious purring motor on the thrum.
> While cities sleep and fortunes fail
> Cats are always on the prowl.
> Now, about your feline? Do you know where it is now?

"Quick cat" is an example of alliteration, as are "never" and "know," "keeps" and "cautious," "cities" and "sleep." Alliterative effect occurs in the second line, with the *s* sound and repeated *p*'s.

When a device such as alliteration is pursued for its own sake, the effect draws so much attention to itself that the poem suffers. Such may be the case with Edgar Allan Poe's "The Bells" (though he takes alliteration to such extremes that the result is sort of interestingly insane).

Hear the sledges with the bells—
Silver bells!
What a world of merriment their melody foretells!
How they tinkle, tinkle, tinkle,
In the icy air of night!
While the stars, that oversprinkle
All the heavens, seem to twinkle
With a crystalline delight;
Keeping time, time, time,
In a sort of Runic rhyme,
To the tintinnabulation that so musically wells
From the bells, bells, bells, bells,
Bells, bells, bells—
From the jingling and the tinkling of the bells.

Because alliteration is such a strong device and so evident when used, it is best reserved for moments when it seems almost unavoidable. Used well, the alliterative effect builds slowly, and the reader becomes aware of it gradually, if at all. In one of Hayden Carruth's "Paragraphs," we can see alliteration at its best.

. . . Yet my call
came a whisper, my sentence an arabesque,
my song falsetto. Put the book back on the shelf.
Gone goodness. Dear mother, dead father, what burlesque
of feeling phonied us, what made you make me hate myself?

An interesting exercise is to look for examples of alliteration in poems you have already written, and underline or circle all such instances. Does the alliteration serve as a subtle means of holding the poem together? Where it does not, you might consider alternatives. And, you may well find instances where unintended alliteration has added magic to your work.

A special potential of sound is its ability to guide what we write. Close yourself in a closet, if you are sensitive about alarming someone, and, with the light on, read aloud a list of all the consonants, slowly making the *sounds* (not pronouncing the name of the letter). Exaggerate the mouth and facial movements required to utter these sounds. Do some of these facial movements, exaggerated, become facial *expressions*? Is there a "gangster" consonant, a "sad" consonant, a "loving" sound? Many writers find that they can best create dialogue for their characters by screwing up their faces and making themselves look as they imagine their characters to look. Then, as they speak, the words are emanating from the character, not from the writer or the narrator.

Employing the "voice" of a character in your poems, indeed employing two or three voices in a single poem, can add a depth and variety to your work beyond expectation, especially if you do not provide obvious indication that the voice, or speaker, has changed.

Alliteration might be useful in helping you find a certain type of character or voice, and you might even decide to make a certain consonant your character's favorite letter. But beware of allowing the letter to appear so often in the final draft of your writing that its presence as an alliterative device becomes distracting. Use it all you want in the early drafts, but revise with an eye toward making it subtle.

Alphabet Poem

The alphabet poem is one that uses the letters of the alphabet as points of departure for lines or whole poems. This can be done in several ways.

One method is to select a single letter of the alphabet, look at it, let its appearance suggest images and ideas, and write them down, as e.e. cummings (1894-1962) did with the letter *i*:

who are you, little i

(five or six years old)
peering from some high

window at the gold
of november sunset

and feeling: that if day
has to become night

this is a beautiful way

In this case, the dot in the letter *i* reminds cummings of a child's head. His imagination adds the details: where the child is, and what the child is doing and feeling.

In the following example, Dawn Olmo (fourth grade) saw the up-turned, open beak of a baby bird in the letter *M*:

Who Are You, Hungry M?

A baby bird chirping
for a worm
and never getting fed?
You're trying to
sing and beg
for one.
But you're still
not getting anything
until you look up
in sorrow.

12

Another type of alphabet poem uses the letters *a-z* or *z-a* as the first letters of the twenty-six words in the poem:

> Zachery yelled x-rays
> while Valerie unkindly tore sweatsocks,
> running quickly
> passing objectionable nitwit money
> laughing & killing;
> Janet's illness hastily got funny.
> especially delirious
> causing beautiful amnesia.
> — *Kismani Andrade (fourth grade)*

Notice that an extra word *(&)* was snuck in there.

Another type of alphabet poem makes every (or almost every) word in a line begin with the same letter:

> Ann announced an aardvark accidentally ate another awkward
> aardvark.
> Barry banned Beaker Bean's banker bat.
> Cats courageously cooked canned, cut dogs.
> Debonnaire Darcy danced delightfully to death.
> — *Joomi Park, Lindsey Leighland, and Darci Evans*
> *(fourth grade)*

And so on. Notice how the necessity of repeating the letter seems to create bizarre scenes. The repeating of the same letter also causes an effect called alliteration. Lines with excessive alliteration can be quite funny when said aloud.

Another type of alphabet poem is represented by Edward Lear's "Alphabet":

> A   tumbled down, and hurt his Arm, against a bit of wood.
> B   said, 'My Boy, O! do not cry; it cannot do you good!'
> C   said, 'A Cup of Coffee hot can't do you any harm.'
> D   said, 'A Doctor should be fetched, and he would cure the
>   arm.'
> E   said, 'An Egg beat up with milk would quickly make him
>   well.'

F   said, 'A Fish, if broiled, might cure, if only by the smell.'

G   said, 'Green Gooseberry fool, the best of cures I hold.'

H   said, 'His Hat should be kept on, to keep him from the cold.'

I   said, 'Some Ice upon his head will make him better soon.'

J   said, 'Some Jam, if spread on bread, or given in a spoon!'

K   said, 'A Kangaroo is here, — this picture let him see.'

L   said, 'A Lamp pray keep alight, to make some barley tea.'

M   said, 'A Mulberry or two might give him satisfaction.'

N   said, 'Some Nuts, if rolled about, might be a slight attraction.'

O   said, 'An Owl might make him laugh, if only it would wink.'

P   said, 'Some Poetry might be read aloud, to make him think.'

Q   said, 'A Quince I recommend, — a Quince, or else a Quail.'

R   said, 'Some Rats might make him move, if fastened by their tail.'

S   said, 'A Song should now be sung, in hopes to make him laugh!'

T   said, 'A Turnip might avail, if sliced or cut in half!'

U   said, 'An Urn, with water hot, place underneath his chin!'

V   said, 'I'll stand upon a chair, and play a Violin!'

W   said, 'Some Whiskey-Whizzgigs fetch, some marbles and a ball!'

X   said, 'Some double XX ale would be the best of all!'

Y   said, 'Some Yeast mixed up with salt would make a perfect plaster!'

Z   said, 'Here is a box of Zinc! Get in, my little master!
We'll shut you up! We'll nail you down!
    We will, my little master!
We think we've all heard quite enough of this your sad disaster!'

See also: ALLITERATION, WORD PLAY.

Assonance

("ASS-uh-nance")

Assonance (from a Latin word meaning "to correspond to in sound") is the repetition without rhyme of vowel sounds in stressed syllables. It usually creates a soothing effect in poems. Note that it is easier to "stretch" a vowel sound so that it is almost hummed than it is to make a consonant sound last more than a moment. This is because the formation of consonant sounds relies on a kind of verbal percussion: the lips meet to pop off a *p*, the tongue taps the palate for the *t*, or bounces near the teeth to make a *d*. Note that, to make the vowel *sounds, A E I O U*, the speaker need not move the mouth at all once it is set, although to pronounce the **letter** *u* (as opposed to making the **sound** a *u* represents) one has to constrict the mouth slightly to form the sound of a consonant *y*, as in "you."

In some poems, assonance is used as a substitute for true rhyme. In William Shakespeare's sonnets, scholars have found only two examples of "impure" or "slant" rhyme, and both of these make good use of assonance. Here are those two, rare departures from a strict rhyme scheme.

> Is it thy will thy image should keep open
> My heavy eyelids to the weary night?
> Dost thou desire my slumbers should be broken
> While shadows like to thee do mock my sight?
> *—From "Sonnet 61"*

Although "open" and "broken" a perfect rhyme do not make, they certainly sound alike, and this is because assonance is established by the long *o* they have in common.

> Oh, that our night of woe might have remembered
> My deepest sense, how hard true sorrow hits,
> And soon to you, as you to me, then tendered
> The humble salve which wounded bosoms fits!
> *—From "Sonnet 120"*

Assonance in this sonnet is established between "remembered" and "tendered."

Good poets often find ways to mix assonance with alliteration, fashioning a poem that often seems "tight," because the sounds have such a harmonious effect. Here is Shakespeare's twelfth sonnet. See how many examples of assonance and alliteration you can find.

When I do count the clock that tells the time
And see the brave day sunk in hideous night,
When I behold the violet past prime
And sable curls all silvered o'er with white;
When lofty trees I see barren of leaves
Which erst from heat did canopy the herd,
And summer's green all girded up in sheaves,
Borne on the bier with white and bristly beard—
Then of beauty do I question make,
That thou among the wastes of time must go,
Since sweets and beauties do themselves forsake
And die as fast as they see others grow.
    And nothing 'gainst Time's scythe can make defense
    Save breed, to brave him when he takes thee hence.

(Note that "breed" means "offspring"; "brave" means "taunt.")

Ballad

The ballad originated as a folksong that tells an exciting story. It is a popular poetic form all over the world. People make up and sing ballads in cultures that have no reading or writing, as well as in those that do.

In the English-speaking world, some of the oldest ballads come from the wild and desolate "border country" between England and Scotland where families lived in clans many miles apart from each other. Fairies, witches, ghosts, and other supernatural beings were believed to be alive and operating in this culture. Many of the ballads tell stories about fatal relationships: between lovers, between family members, between clans, or between people and these supernatural beings. Just as sensational or "bad" news gets the most attention in our newspapers and on TV today, so the most tragic and strange stories of that time inspired the making of ballads. For ballads are a way of communicating the strong feelings provoked by such dramatic human events. The following ballad is based on a personal rather than a collective experience, but its story concerns the universal mysteries of love and death, and so affects us all. The words go like this (remember, it would have been sung to an eerily catchy tune):

The Unquiet Grave

The wind doth blow today, my love,
    And a few small drops of rain.
I never had but one true-love,
    In cold grave she was lain.

I'll do as much for my true-love
    As any young man may,
I'll sit and mourn all at her grave
    For a twelvemonth and a day.

The twelvemonth and a day being up,
   The dead began to speak:
Oh who sits weeping on my grave,
   And will not let me sleep?

'Tis I, my love, sits on your grave,
   And will not let you sleep,
For I crave one kiss of your clay-cold lips,
   And that is all I seek.

You crave one kiss of my clay-cold lips,
   But my breath smells earthy strong.
If you have one kiss of my clay-cold lips,
   Your time will not be long.

'Tis down in yonder garden green,
   Love, where we used to walk,
The finest flower that ere was seen
   Is withered to a stalk.

The stalk is withered dry, my love,
   So will our hearts decay;
So make yourself content, my love,
   Until you are called away.

Traditional British ballads are written in such four-line stanzas; lines 1 and 3 have four beats; lines 2 and 4 have three beats and rhyme.

When a society is going through a time of many changes, a popular energy often arises and expresses its opinions through ballads. In the early part of this century, before there were labor unions to protect the rights of workers from unsympathetic employers, there were often confrontations between the working people and the company police ("the copper boss thug-men," in this case), employed to keep the workers in line. The following ballad — a variation on the traditional ballad — tells the story of a malicious prank played by some of the company police that became a tragedy for the workers:

The 1913 Massacre

Take a trip with me in nineteen thirteen,
To Calumet, Michigan in the copper country,
I'll take you to a place called "Italian Hall,"
Where miners are having their big Christmas ball.

18

I will take you in a door and up a high stairs,
Singing and dancing is heard everywhere,
I will let you shake hands with the people you see,
And watch the kids dance 'round the big Christmas tree.

You ask about work and you ask about pay,
They'll tell you they make less than a dollar a day,
Working the copper claims, risking their lives,
So it's fun to spend Christmas with children and wives.

There's talking and laughing and songs in the air,
And the spirit of Christmas is there everywhere,
Before you know it you're friends with us all,
And you're dancing around and around in the hall.

Well a little girl sits down by the Christmas tree lights,
To play the piano, so you gotta keep quiet,
To hear all this fun you would not realize,
That the copper boss thug-men are milling outside.

The copper boss thugs stuck their heads in the door,
One of them yelled and screamed, "There's a fire!"
A lady, she hollered, "There's no such a thing,
Keep on with your party, there's no such a thing."

A few people rushed, and it was only a few,
"It's just the thugs and the scabs fooling you."
A man grabbed his daughter and carried her down,
But the thugs held the door and he could not get out.

And then others followed, a hundred or more,
But most everybody remained on the floor,
The gun-thugs they laughed at their murderous joke,
While the children were smothered on the stairs by the door.

Such a terrible sight I never did see,
We carried our children back up to their tree,
The scabs outside still laughed at their spree,
And the children that died there were seventy-three.

The piano played a slow funeral tune,
The town was lit up by a cold Christmas moon
The parents they cried and the miners they moaned,
"See what your greed for money has done."
    — *Woody Guthrie*

Other American ballads include "John Henry" and "The Streets of Laredo," a cowboy ballad.

When the old Scottish and English ballads were rediscovered by poets and scholars in the eighteenth century, poets began to write literary ballads. These ballads are made to be read, not sung, but they use the narrative and dramatic style and rhythmic structure of the old ballads. Some of them (such as Coleridge's "The Rime of the Ancient Mariner") are variations on the ballad.

Whether oral or written, the best ballads have precise and startling "images" that sometimes arise and take the reader/hearer directly into the story. In "The Unquiet Grave," there's the gloomy image of the dead lover's "clay cold lips," and in "The 1913 Massacre," there is the warm and friendly description of the Christmas party with its bright details: "Well a little girl sits down by the Christmas tree lights/ To play the piano so you gotta keep quiet." Through such images we feel the situation and troubles of the ballad characters as if they were our own. So, in addition to the musical nature of the ballad's form, there is a visual aspect to the story, which develops rich and emotion-charged mental pictures (images). These strike our imagination in such a way that the story comes to life for us with something like the power of a recollected dream.

Ballade
("bah-LAHD")

The ballade is a fairly complicated verse form with a heavy stress on rhyme. It is an old form, French in origin, and although poets of other nationalities have used it, it is the French who have had the most success with it. The word *ballade* comes from an Old French word that means "a dancing-song."

The most common shape the ballade takes is that of three stanzas, followed by an *envoi* (a short final stanza) that addresses an important person and sums up the point of the poem. The number of lines in the envoi is always half the number of lines of one of the stanzas.

Usually each stanza of the ballade consists of eight lines. The three stanzas always use the same rhymes (although not necessarily the same words) and always follow the same rhyme scheme: *ababbcbC*. The last line *(C)* is the same for all three stanzas and it is also always the last line of the envoi, whose scheme is always *bcbC*. The rhyme scheme for a whole ballade is thus *ababbcbC ababbcbC ababbcbC bcbC*.

There are some variations on the ballade. Sometimes the stanzas consist of ten lines instead of eight. Then the rhyme scheme for the stanzas is *ababbccdcD*. The envoi will be five lines and the rhyme scheme for it will be *ccdcD*. Other variations for the ballade include a twelve-line stanza with a six-line envoi and the double ballade, which has six stanzas of eight or ten or twelve lines but no concluding envoi.

The ballade reached its peak as a form in France during the fourteenth and fifteenth centuries. Such poets as Guillaume de Machaut, Christine de Pisan, and Charles d'Orleans were distinguished for theirs, but the poet considered the master of the form is the mysterious François Villon. He was a student and poet who became a thief, living romantically and violently. One of his most famous ballades is called "Ballade of the Hanged."

The following excerpt from Villon's "Ballade," in which he talks about the world that leads him to steal, is a good example of the form. It's written in ten-line stanzas, so the form is *ababbccdcD,* with *D* as the concluding line of all the stanzas as well as the five-line envoi. The English translation by Galway Kinnell is a literal one with no rhyme, so to follow the form you'll have to look at the French while using the English to get the sense.

Je meurs de seuf auprès de la fontaine,
Chault comme feu et tremble dent à dent,
En mon païs suis en terre loingtaine,
Lez ung brasier frissone tout ardent,
Nu comme ung ver, vestu en président,
Je ris en pleurs et attens sans espoir,
Confort reprens en triste desespoir,
Je m'esjouis et n'ay plaisir aucun,
Puissant je suis sans force et sans povoir,
Bien recueully, debouté de chascun.

Envoi:
Prince clement, or vous plaise scavoir
Que j'entens moult et n'ay sens ne scavoir,
Parcial suis a toutes loys commun,
Que fais je plus? Quoy? Les gaiges ravoir!
Bien recuelly, debouté de chascun.

*

I die of thirst beside the fountain,
Hot as a fire I'm shaking tooth on tooth,
In my own country I'm in a distant land,
Beside the blaze I'm shivering in flames,
Naked as a worm, dressed like a president,
I laugh in tears and hope despairingly,
I cheer up in sad despair,
I'm joyful and nothing gives me pleasure,
I'm strong and haven't any force or power,
Warmly welcomed, rebuffed by everyone.

Envoi:
Merciful Prince, may it please you to know
I understand much and have no sense of learning,
A rare bird, I'm common before the law,
What's left to do? Set eyes on my pawned goods again!
Warmly welcomed, rebuffed by everyone.

In writing a ballade, the most important thing to keep under control is the rhyme scheme. You don't want to make your rhymes too simple (dark/bark, moon/spoon, love/dove) nor do you want to make them too complicated (how many words are there that rhyme with *orange*?). Find words/rhymes that make sense to use, are not too obvious, and which you can have fun with. You should also remember that in writing your envoi, although it isn't necessary, it is a traditional part of the form to begin with a salutation (see, for example, how Villon uses "Merciful Prince").

You can write ballades about almost anything but, considering the rhymes and the envoi's salute, it might be most interesting to direct your poem to a specific person and/or occasion. For example, you could use the ballade form to create a poem-as-gift, maybe a birthday present. Or, if you want to have more fun, you might use the poem satirically, the way Villon does. You can direct it at someone who stands for a cause (political or otherwise) you don't agree with.

Blank Verse

Blank verse took its name from the fact that poets and their audiences once expected every line of poetry to end with a rhyme word. When English poets in the late sixteenth century began to write in a ten-syllable line influenced by unrhymed Italian poems, a "blank" (unrhymed) word was used to conclude each line. This new poetry, which also usually had five major stresses or accents in each line, slowly became known as the *blank* verse — the poetry that didn't have lines that ended in rhymes.

Henry Howard, Earl of Surrey (1517?–1547), is credited with being the first poet in our language to use this new verse line. It appeared in the two books he translated from Virgil's Latin epic poem, *The Aeneid.* Sometimes he used it with great skill. These lines, from Book II, introduce the battle of Laocoön, the sea-god Neptune's priest, with a sea-monster. (Surrey's original spelling and punctuation have been retained, but explanatory notes in italics have been added between the lines):

Whiles Laocon, that chosen was by lot
While   Laocoön
Neptunus priest, did sacrifice a bull
Neptune's
Before the holy altar, sodenly
     suddenly
From Tenedon, behold, in circles great
 Tenedos
By the calme seas come fletyng adders twayne
     floating   serpents   two
Which plied towardes the shore (I lothe to tell)
      loathe
With rered brest lift up above the seas,
  reared   breast
Whoes bloody crestes aloft the waves were seen
Whose
The hinder parte swamme hidden in the flood;
  hind   *water*

Their grisly backes were linked manifold.
With sound of broken waves they gate the strand,
reached   shore
With gloing eyen, tained with blood and fire;
glowing eyes
Whoes waltring tongs did lick their hissing mouths
wavering   tongues
We fled away, our face the blood forsoke.
forsook

At other times, Surrey's line could be clunky, mechanical, so lacking in word-music as to be called "wooden." Thomas Sackville and Thomas Norton abandoned rhymed drama to use the new line in their play *Gorboduc*. But in the hands of Christopher Marlowe (1564-1593) blank verse became a first-rate medium for poetry. It was as if, all by himself, the poet-playwright had invented a new musical instrument—a whole symphony orchestra, many critics would say— out of the crude instruments left by the writers who had used the line before him. Below are some lines from the final soliloquy in *Doctor Faustus,* as Faustus begs to be saved from the Devil coming to claim his soul. The old spellings are less troublesome if you read these lines aloud:

The starres moove still, time runs, the clocke wil strike,
The divel wil come, and Faustus must be damnd.
O Ile leape up to my God: who pulles me down?
See see where Christs blood streames in the firmament.
One drop would save my soule, halfe a drop, ah my Christ.
Ah rend not my heart for naming of my Christ,
Yet wil I call on him: oh spare me *Lucifer*!
Where is it now? tis gone: And see where God
Stretcheth out his arme, and bends his irefull browes:
Moutaines and hilles, come, come, and fall on me,
And hide me from the heavy wrath of God.
No, no.
Then will I headlong runne into the earth:
Earth gape. O no, it wil not harbour me:
You starres that raignd at my nativitie,
Whose influence hath alotted death and hel,
Now draw up Faustus like a foggy mist,

Into the intrailes of yon labring cloude
That when you vomite foorth into the ayre,
My limbes may issue from your smoaky mouthes,
So that my soule may but ascend to heaven. . . .

With the plays of William Shakespeare (1564-1616), however, blank verse achieved even greater expressive power. If Marlowe had invented a new orchestra, Shakespeare used it to create symphonies. There is nothing he cannot make his ten-syllable line do, be it a slow, stately march or a whip-like attack of crackling words. He can start a line, plunge it ahead, stop it suddenly, break it off, then pick up speed, or in a moment creep along at will. He well understood the connection between spoken English and its dramatic use, and this is why his characters sound so "natural" to us, even at a distance of almost 400 years, and even though they are "speaking poetry."

The blank verse line has remained a favorite of poets. After Shakespeare, dozens of important dramatists used it, and when the English drama died out, the line reappeared with new vigor and complexity in immense masterpieces like John Milton's *Paradise Lost* (1667). William Wordsworth carried the blank verse line forward in many of his poems, such as the long autobiographical poem *The Prelude*. In doing so, Wordsworth brought blank verse (and poetry itself) closer to everyday speech and the concerns of common people. The "dramatic monologues" (dramatic speeches spoken by one character) created by Robert Browning in the nineteenth century added new power to the line.

Modern poets have continued to use the blank verse line. Perhaps its master among the "classical moderns" of the twentieth century was Robert Frost, who found poetry in the conversation of native New Englanders. Many of Frost's best poems are in blank verse — "The Death of the Hired Man" and "Mending Wall" among them.

A good way to begin writing blank verse is to practice writing a ten-syllable line. At first, many of your lines won't have five stresses — five syllables that are strongly accented. Don't worry about that at the start. (If you do, you'll spend all your time getting *one* line right, and that isn't the point.) Write the lines in your own speaking voice, and keep a fingertip syllable count. Some of your lines will be eight or nine syllables long; others will be eleven or twelve syllables. Here's an example, written quickly:

I want to begin to speak to you
about how blank verse ought to be written.
Open your window and look outside. See
the people passing by, the shiny cars
as they zoom along the streets, honking horns.

These are respectable, if not brilliant, lines of blank verse. They keep the feel of natural language. By tinkering around with the syllables and accents, the lines can be "regularized" — given ten syllables and an iambic (- /) beat. "I want to tell you everything I know" would be perhaps a better first line. Most blank verse being written today by poets is "loose." It *almost* follows the rules. As you get better at writing blank verse — and you'll have to read and write a lot of it to do that — you'll naturally write a "tighter" line.

Blank verse seems inseparably joined to drama and story-telling. In fact, it is hard to think of examples of it, reaching all the way back to Surrey's translations, that *don't* tell stories.

See also: FOOT.

Blues Poem

Blues poetry came from the musical form known as "the blues."
The blues is American, but its roots are in African music. The earliest
American ancestors of the blues were work songs and "field hollers"
(a musical form of talk among slaves) that came out of the Deep
South. The blues were first made popular around 1900 by W.C.
Handy, who wrote the famous "St. Louis Blues." Much American
popular music — rhythm and blues, rock and roll, disco, rap, and jazz
— is drawn from the blues.

There are two types of blues poems. The first type has no particular form, but has the content typical of the blues. Here is an example of this type of blues, by Langston Hughes, the first American
poet to use blues successfully:

Evil

Looks like what drives me crazy
Don't have no effect on you —
But I'm gonna keep on at it
Till it drives you crazy, too.

The second type of blues poem is one that has blues content *and* the
structure of the old blues songs. Here's an example, again by
Hughes:

Morning After

I was so sick last night I
Didn't hardly know my mind.
So sick last night I
Didn't hardly know my mind.
I drunk some bad licker that
Almost made me blind.

Had a dream last night I
Thought I was in hell.
I drempt last night I
Thought I was in hell.
Woke up and looked around me—
Babe, your mouth was open like a well.

I said, Baby! Baby!
Please don't snore so loud.
Baby! Please!
Please don't snore so loud.
You jest like a little bit o' woman but you
Sound like a great big crowd.

Notice the repetition of lines (with slight variations). The traditional blues stanza consisted of three lines: a first line repeated (often with variations) as the second line, then a different line, all rhyming, as in:

In the evenin', in the evenin', momma, when the sun go down,
In the evenin', darlin', I declare, when the sun go down,
Yes, it's so lonesome, so lonesome, when the one you love is not
    around.

In "Morning After," Langston Hughes uses this same form, but he breaks the three long lines into six shorter ones.

As its names suggests, blues songs are about hopelessness, grief, and loss. But they are more than that. As Ralph Ellison says, the blues "at once express the agony of life and the possibility of conquering it through sheer toughness of spirit." Ellison also says that the blues do not offer a solution to the human condition. They do, however, offer a resolution: an acceptance of pain, sickness, and death that is marked by grace and irony, and a defiant decision to preserve the human spirit. And as Hughes' "Morning After" shows, a blues poem can even express the humor of a bad situation. Generally, though, they are more serious:

As Befits a Man

I don't mind dying—
But I'd hate to die all alone!
I want a dozen pretty women
To holler, cry, and moan.

29

I don't mind dying
But I want my funeral to be fine:
A row of long, tall mamas
Fainting, fanning, and crying.

I want a fish-tail hearse
And sixteen fish-tail cars,
A big brass band
And a whole truck load of flowers.

When they let me down,
Down into the clay,
I want the women to holler:
Please don't take him away!
    Ow-ooo-oo-o!
Don't take Daddy away!

To write a blues poem, think of something that depresses you.
Some typical subjects are "I ain't got no money blues," "I ain't got
nothing but D's on my report card blues," and "My parents are driv-
ing me crazy blues." To get a better feel for the blues form, you
might also listen to a lot of traditional blues songs by Lightnin'
Hopkins, Robert Johnson, Furry Lewis, Blind Lemon Jefferson, Big
Bill Broonzy, and others. And remember, in blues poems the language can be "down home"; for example, it ain't bad to say "ain't."

Bouts-Rimés
("boo re-MAY")

Bouts-rimés is French for "rhymed ends." A bouts-rimés poem is created by one person's making up a list of rhymed words and giving it to another person, who in turn writes the lines that end with those rhymes, in the same order in which they were given. For example, one person writes down *tanned, jump, fanned, lump, reading, lawn, misleading, yawn, yoyo, death, no-no, breath, France* and *pants* for another person to use as rhymes, as in:

> Getting burnt, evaporated, bleached, or tanned
> By the sun ain't no way to jump.
> I'd rather plop in shadow, be fanned
> By some geisha girl, and lay around like a proverbial lump.
>
> I'm not that hot for so-called good reading;
> I just crave a cool drink on a bluegreen lawn.
> I mean, don't let me be misleading:
> Where I'm at is sorta like the center of a yawn.
>
> You now, excitement's like being a yoyo—
> I don't wanna beat the subject to death,
> And it isn't that repetition ain't no no-no,
> But the last thing I hope to be is out of breath.
>
> So let somebody else go lost-generate all over France,
> Or fly to the moon, discover Africa, some damn hotshot
>   smartypants.
>   —*Jack Collom*

The weirder the list of rhymes, the more challenging it is to make them make sense together and seem natural. On the other hand, the author might want to create a poem that doesn't make sense (see NONSENSE VERSE). Either way, the bouts-rimés poem requires wit and mental agility.

31

Bouts-rimés are said to have been invented by a seventeenth-century French poet named Dulot. They were very popular throughout the eighteenth and nineteenth centuries. In 1864 Alexandre Dumas, the author of *The Three Musketeers,* invited all the poets of France to fill in the lines for a set of selected rhymes. The next year he published the result: 350 poems by as many poets, all with the exact same rhymes. Why not do the same with a group of friends, a class, a school, a city?

Calligram
("CAL-ih-gram")

The word *calligram* comes from the French *calligramme,* itself derived from the Greek *calli* and *gramma*, which together mean "beautiful writing."

The French poet Guillaume Apollinaire was aware of this meaning when he invented the French form of the word and used it as the title of his book of poems *Calligrammes* (1918). In this book, he published poems that didn't look like poems: his calligrams had words and lines in new combinations and shapes. Some of the calligrams had a shape that related to their subject, as in "It's Raining" (figure 1). This poem is about how the rain reminds the poet of his past: women, marvelous encounters, horses and the towns suggested by their neighing, and how the path of the raindrop suggests lines that bind us to the sky and our past. But notice how different the poem would look and feel if it were printed the way poems usually are:

> It's raining women's voices as if they were dead even in memory
> it's also raining you marvelous encounters of my life O droplets
> and these rearing clouds start neighing an entire world of
>   auricular cities
> listen if it's raining while regret and disdain weep an ancient
>   music
> listen to the falling lines that bind you high and low

It's not the same, is it?

Apollinaire wrote quite a few of these poems whose shape reflects their subject, poems shaped like a valentine, a star, a pistol, the Eiffel Tower, a necktie, a carnation, and so on. In doing so, he was in a worldwide tradition that, in the West, goes back at least as far as the ancient Greeks, the tradition of what is called "shaped poetry" or "pattern poetry." The English poet George Herbert (1593-1633) wrote two famous shaped poems, "Easter Wings" and "The Altar." In Lewis Carroll's *Alice's Adventures in Wonderland,* the mouse-tail might be considered a shaped poem.

33

IT'S RAINING

I
t'
s
raining women's voices as if they were dead even in memory

it'
s
also raining you marvelous encounters of my life O droplets

and these rearing clouds start neighing an entire world of auricular cities

listen if it's raining while regret and disdain weep an ancient music

listen to the falling lines that bind you high and low

--Guillaume Apollinaire

Figure 1

34

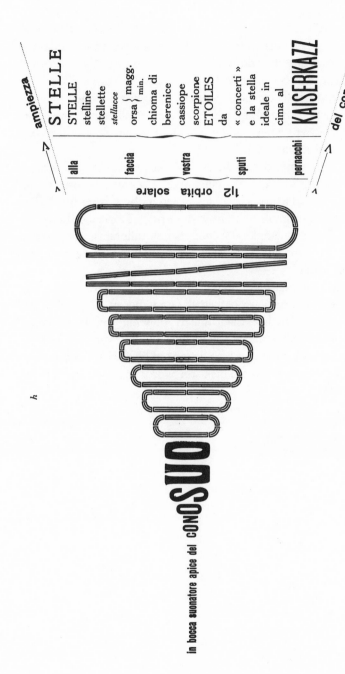

TARANTELLA estensione TUTTA ITALIA

Figure 2

— *Francesco Cangiullo*

Apollinaire's calligrams were a little different. Some of them were *not* in the shape of a particular thing: the lines were tilted around the page or with words in various different sizes. In this, Apollinaire had been influenced by Stephane Mallarmé's poem "A Throw of the Dice Will Never Abolish Chance," an astoundingly experimental poem published in 1897. But ultimately Apollinaire's calligrams came from his desire to invent a new kind of writing that he felt was necessary for expressing modern life.

At the same time, certain Italian and Russian artists and writers were experimenting along the same lines. They were known as the "Futurists." The Futurists were interested in "words set free." Figure 2 shows an example of a Futurist poem by Francesco Cangiullo (1916). In all these examples — shaped poems, calligrams, and Futurist words set free — the poem has taken a step toward turning itself into a visual art work.

To write a calligram, you might first want to choose a shape that has a clear outline, such as a basketball or a window. Then fill in the shape with words and lines that come to you when you think about a particular basketball game or a particular window you look out of. Or you might want the words to be spoken by the basketball or the window. Remember, you can make the words any size, style, or color you want.

See also: CONCRETE POEM.

Canto
("CAN-toe")

Cantos are the divisions or shorter sections of longer poetic works. We can think of them as being the poetic equivalents of the chapters of a novel. Originally, when poetry was sung—the word *canto* comes from a Latin word that means "song" — the division into cantos would give the singer a chance to rest before proceeding to the next part. But more importantly (and this is especially true after poetry stops being sung), the dividing of the work into cantos becomes a practical way for the poet to examine one particular aspect or variation of the larger theme or plot of his or her poem.

Dante's *Divine Comedy* is a good example of how poets have used cantos in the organization of their poems. Dante divides his 13th-century masterpiece into three parts, with a total of one hundred cantos. The first canto describes how the whole work has come to be written. Next come the thirty-three cantos of the "Inferno," the thirty-three of the "Purgatory" and the thirty-three of the "Paradise." Dante's cantos are too long to quote here, but even a simple summary of the first few reveals how he used them to construct his epic.

Canto I—Dante introduces himself, his life; he talks about his visions and meets the Roman poet Virgil, who will be his guide through Hell.

Canto II—The *Inferno* begins with the appearance of Beatrice, who convinces Dante to go with Virgil; he agrees and the journey starts.

Canto III—At the gates of Hell, meeting those who wait outside.

Canto IV—The first circle (level) of Hell, the poets and Virtuous Heathens.

Canto V—The second circle, Minos, the sin of lust, Paolo and Francesca.

Canto VI—The third circle, the sin of gluttony, Cerberus, Ciacco.

The above example shows fairly neat divisions of both action and theme, one canto per moment, per circle, etc. As the descent into Hell and Dante's spiritual understanding continue, though, the structure of the cantos becomes more complicated because the fates of the sinners and the implications of the sins become more complicated. Still, Dante's cantos hold to a fairly straightforward pattern: though he may remain in a circle for more than one canto, each canto explores a specific aspect of that circle and the sinners and sins punished there. Dante may use what he learns from a previous canto to explore a new point, but he will not rehash the old point.

Byron, Ariosto, and Pope are other poets who divided their long works into cantos. In the twentieth century, the most important poet to use the canto was the American poet Ezra Pound. Pound spent much of his life writing a large work known as *The Cantos*. Initially, he meant his epic to mirror Dante's and to consist of exactly one hundred cantos, but he expanded his conception of the work so that, when he died in 1972, there were 114 cantos completed, with several in fragments and more planned. Written in a number of languages, including English, Chinese, Greek, Italian, French, and Spanish, at once difficult to read and inspiring, Pound's *Cantos* stand as a massive visionary epic, in which he writes poetry and then collages it with hundreds of other texts, poetic, historical, journalistic, economic, and scientific. Through this radical mixing of texts, Pound was trying to examine ancient and modern life and, in so doing, to find an underlying system of universal constants that might explain and even predict the development of civilization.

You don't need to be as ambitious as Pound or Dante to write a work in cantos. Any poetic work that is longer than several pages can be divided into parts that are individual and independent and still reflect the broader theme or plot of the work. For example, if you are writing a long work about a certain character and that character's adventures, a model similar to Dante's could be employed in which the various cantos tell different stages of plot and character development. If you are talking about an idea, a plan that follows a philosophical/historical development similar to Pound's might hold some clues as to how to proceed.

See also: EPIC.

Canzone
("can-ZONE-ay")

The term *canzone* covers a wide variety of verse forms, but they all have in common their song-like nature. The word *canzone* is an Italian word derived from the Latin *cantio*, meaning "song."

In the thirteenth century, the poets of Italy, Spain, and France traveled from court to court composing and performing lyrical poems that they called canzones. The lengths of the poems and their rhyme schemes and complex metrical patterns varied greatly. Canzones were most often written in praise of beauty, or about love, philosophy, or metaphysics (the nature of being and the origin of the world).

The Italian poet Dante coined the phrase "dolce stil nuovo" to describe the style of the canzone: "a sweet new style." Dante's book *La Vita Nuova (The New Life)* contains the most famous canzone, whose last stanza goes (in English):

> Dear Song, I know thou wilt hold gentle speech
> With many ladies, when I send thee forth:
> Wherefore, (being mindful that thou hadst thy birth
> From Love, and art a modest, simple child,)
> Whomso thou meetest, say thou this to each:
> "Give me good speed! To her I wend along
> In whose much strength my weakness is made strong."
> And if, i' the end, thou wouldst not be beguiled
> Of all thy labour, seek not the defiled
> And common sort; but rather choose to be
> Where man and woman dwell in courtesy.
> So to the road thou shalt be reconciled,
> And find the lady, and with the lady, Love.
> Commend thou me to each, as doth behove.
>   — *Translated by D.G. Rossetti*

La Vita Nuova is a book about Dante's love for a woman named Beatrice. It is written in both poetry (sonnets and canzones) and prose. In the prose sections of the book, Dante not only tells the history of his love for Beatrice but also analyzes his own poems line by line.

Canzones by the twelfth- and thirteenth-century Italian poets Arnaut Daniel and Guido Cavalcanti have been made famous in English in the twentieth century because they were translated by the American poet Ezra Pound.

To write a canzone these days, you must find a complicated and challenging form that you think is right for answering questions of love, beauty, and why we exist. Then set the poem to music, and do it in a sweet new style.

Cento

("SEN-toe")

The word *cento* comes from the Latin word meaning "patchwork," as in "patchwork quilt." The cento is a poem made entirely of pieces from poems by other authors. Centos can be rhymed or unrhymed, short or long. Here is one example by John Ashbery:

To a Waterfowl

Where, like a pillow on a bed
I come to pluck your berries harsh and crude
Where through the Golden Coast, and groves of orange and citron
And one clear call for me
My genial spirits fail
The desire of the moth for the star
When first the College Rolls receive his name.

Too happy, happy tree
Here, where men sit and hear each other groan.
Forget this rotten world, and unto thee
Go, for they call you, Shepherd, from the hill
And the eye travels down to Oxford's towers.

Calm was the day, and through the trembling air
Coffee and oranges in a sunny chair
And she also to use newfangleness...
Why cannot the Ear be closed to its own destruction?
Last noon beheld them full of lusty life,
Unaffected by "the march of events",
Never until the mankind making
From harmony, from heavenly harmony
O death, O cover you over with roses and early lilies!
With loaded arms I come, pouring for you
Sunset and evening star
Where roses and white lilies grow.

Go, lovely rose,
This is no country for old men. The young
Midwinter spring is its own season
And a few lilies blow. They that have power to hurt, and will do
    none.
Looking as if she were alive, I call.
The vapours weep their burthen to the ground.
Obscurest night involved the sky
When Loie Fuller, with her Chinese veils
And many a nymph who wreathes her brow with sedge...
We have given our hearts away, a sordid boon!
In drear-nighted December
Ripe apples drop about my head
Who said: two vast and trunkless legs of stone
To throw that faint thin line upon the shore!
O well for the fisherman's boy!
Fra Pandolf's hand
Steady thy laden head across a brook...
With charm of earliest birds; pleasant the sun
Fills the shadows and windy places
Here in the long unlovely street.
Ah, sad and strange as in dark summer dawns
The freezing stream below.
To know the change and feel it...

At that far height, the cold thin atmosphere
Pressed her cold finger closer to her lips
Where the dead feet walked in.
She dwells with Beauty—Beauty that must die,
Or the car rattling o'er the stony street.

Centos go back at least as far as the second century. In the fifth century a cento was written on the life of Christ, with every line borrowed from the Greek poet Homer, whose work was created at least
900 years *before* Christ! Centos continued to be written up until the
seventeenth century, often by churchmen, who could read Latin and
therefore use the classics handed down from Roman times.

Using lines from other sources has been revived in the twentieth
century. T.S. Eliot in "The Waste Land," Ezra Pound in *The Cantos,*
Ted Berrigan in *The Sonnets,* and many others have mixed borrowed
lines with their own work, creating what might be called "collage"

poems. But few modern poets have created true centos, poems made *entirely* of other poets' lines.

A good way to write a cento is to keep a notebook in which you collect lines that strike you. After you've accumulated a bunch, see if they can be arranged to make a new poem.

Another way is to examine the index of first lines in a poetry collection. Sometimes these indexes contain undiscovered centos, as in *An Anthology of New York Poets:*

> Yes, they are alive, and can have those colors,
> Yippee! she is shooting in the harbor! he is jumping
> You approach me carrying a book
> You are bright, tremendous, wow.

Most poetry anthologies have lots of lines beginning with the words *I, you, a,* and *the,* and in the index of first lines these tend to form ready-made centos.

See also: FOUND POEM.

Chant

A chant is a poem of no fixed form, but in which one or more lines are repeated over and over. It is usually meant to be read aloud.

The chant is one of the earliest forms of poetry, dating all the way back to the swirling mists of prehistoric time when cavepeople, sitting around smoky fires, made up magical spells and incantations to protect themselves from wild animals, hurricanes and fires, and to help themselves do well in the hunt, find good-looking mates, and have lots of healthy children.

Chants repeat particular words or phrases over and over because there is something powerful about the repetition of a word or phrase: it adds strength to a poem. Also, the rhythm of the repetition forms a musical beat, one that uses words the way a rock and roll song is driven by its beat.

> Go away now, and leave us alone.
> Go away now, and leave us alone.
> Go away now, and leave us alone.

Try beating that one out on a table top. It should sound like a musical phrase with a strong, rhythmical pattern. To feel it build in intensity, say it aloud seven or eight times, instead of two or three.

Of course, most chants don't repeat just one line over and over. They combine repeated lines or phrases with words and sentences that vary. Blues songs, slave songs, and prison work songs all draw on the ancient form of the chant.

The chant was revived in the 1960s by poets who became interested in exploring the poetry of so-called "primitive" or non-technological civilizations. These poets — such as Jerome Rothenberg, Diane Wakoski, Armand Schwerner, and Anne Waldman — used ancient chants in their public performances and borrowed the chant form to write their own poems.

To write a chant, it helps to come up with a good line you wish to repeat; that is the foundation. Remember that a chant is musical, so make sure that your line or phrase has a lilt or beat that seems musical to you. What do you do next? Why, plunge on into the unknown, remembering that chants have an openness and spontaneity you won't find in a sonnet or a sestina, and lack a predetermined beginning, middle, and end.

Here are two excerpts from interesting chants that will help you get a better idea of the form. The first one is by Frank Mitchell, a Navaho Indian who died in 1967.

War God's Horse Song II

With their voices they are calling me,
With their voices they are calling me!

I am the child of White Shell Woman,
    With their voices they are calling me,
I am the son of the Sun,
    With their voices they are calling me,
I am Turquoise Boy,
    With their voices they are calling me!

From the arching rainbow, turquoise on its outer edge,
    from this side of where it touches the earth,
    With their voices they are calling me,
Now the horses of the Sun-descended-boy,
    With their voices they are calling me!

The turquoise horses are my horses,
    With their voices they are calling me,
Dark stone water jars their hooves,
    With their voices they are calling me,
Arrowheads the frogs of their hooves,
    With their voices they are calling me,
Mirage-stone their striped hooves,
    With their voices they are calling me,
Dark wind their legs,
    With their voices they are calling me,
Cloud shadow their tails,
    With their voices they are calling me,
All precious fabrics their bodies,
    With their voices they are calling me,
Dark cloud their skins,
    With their voices they are calling me,

Scattered rainbow their hair,
    With their voices they are calling me,
Now the Sun rises before them to shine on them,
    With their voices they are calling me!

New moons their cantles,
    With their voices they are calling me,
Sunrays their backstraps,
    With their voices they are calling me,
Rainbows their girths,
    With their voices they are calling me,
They are standing, waiting, on rainbows,
    With their voices they are calling me,
The dark-rain-four-footed-ones, their neck hair falling in a wave,
    With their voices they are calling me!

Sprouting plants their ears,
    With their voices they are calling me,
Great dark stars their eyes,
    With their voices they are calling me,
All kinds of spring waters their faces,
    With their voices they are calling me,
Great shell their lips,
    With their voices they are calling me,
White shell their teeth,
    With their voices they are calling me,
There is flash-lightning in their mouths,
    With their voices they are calling me,
Dark-music sounds from their mouths,
    With their voices they are calling me,
They call out into the dawn,
    With their voices they are calling me,
Their voices reach all the way out to me,
    With their voices they are calling me,
Dawn-pollen is in their mouths,
    With their voices they are calling me,
Flowers and plant-dew are in their mouths,
    With their voices they are calling me!

Sunray their bridles,
    With their voices they are calling me,
To my right arm, beautifully to my hand they come,
    With their voices they are calling me,

This day they become my own horses,
    With their voices they are calling me,
Ever increasing, never diminishing,
    With their voices they are calling me,
My horses of long life and happiness,
    With their voices they are calling me,
I, myself, am the boy of long life and happiness,
    With their voices they are calling me!

With their voices they are calling me,
With their voices they are calling me!
    — Translated by David P. McAllester

The second one, with a more contemporary sound, is by Allan Kaprow.

Raining
    for Olga and Billy Kluver, January 1965

Black highway painted black
Rain washes away

Paper men in bare orchard branches
Rain washes away

Sheets of writing spread over a field
Rain washes away

Little grey boats painted along a gutter
Rain washes away

Naked bodies painted gray
Rain washes away

Bare trees painted red
Rain washes away

See also: BLUES, PERFORMANCE POEM, INSULT POEM.

Cinquain
("SING-cane")

A cinquain (from French meaning "a grouping of five") is either a five-line stanza or a poem in five lines. It can also be called a "quintet." The word *cinquain* was claimed early in the twentieth century by Adelaide Crapsey, a young American poet. She used it as the name of a syllabic verse form she invented.

The cinquain has five lines, with two, four, six, eight, and two syllables, respectively. Rhythmically, a cinquain sometimes moves in iambs (see FOOT), but is not required to. Often the first or last line has two strongly accented syllables. Usually cinquains do not have obvious rhymes; when they do, the effect can be humorous.

Crapsey used her cinquains to capture brief statements and images during the last few years of her life (she died at thirty-six). She also knew the rhythmic possibilities of English too well to stick rigidly to her own pattern, and varied it now and then, as the second example below shows. The first is her best-known poem.

Triad

These be
Three silent things:
The falling snow.. the hour
Before the dawn.. the mouth of one
Just dead.

Laurel in the Berkshires

Sea-foam
And coral! Oh, I'll
Climb the great pasture rocks
And dream me mermaid in the sun's
Gold flood.

There are several things to remember about writing cinquains. First, in any short poem, it's tempting to add extra words to fill out the form, or make it a syrupy saying, some large generality about "life." Most effective cinquains stick to nouns naming objects. Even Crapsey occasionally fell into the trap of piling up adjectives: "Autumnal, evanescent, wan, / The moon." If she hadn't been writing in this form she might have said "a thin November moon." Avoid goo.

Second, if each line sounds "finished" (for example, if each line is a complete phrase), the poem bumps from line-end to line-end and sounds boring, for all its brevity.

Finally, the cinquain should build toward a climax. Notice the sense of suspense at the ends of the next-to-last lines of the examples, and the surprise in the last lines.

Collaboration
("co-lab-or-A-shun")

The word *collaboration* means to work together, "co-labor," from the Latin word *collaborare*.

In the Western world, poets usually envision themselves writing alone (in a room or perhaps on a mountain top), yet for over a thousand years Japanese poets have collaborated in writing the *renga*, a poem written by two or more poets together.

There are many ways to collaborate in poetry:

- Writing alternate lines of a poem, with or without looking at what the other person has written.
- Writing a long work as a whole class or group of people, each contributing to a single subject, such as dreams, memories, or bee stings.
- Writing one poem or a series of poems through the mail, each poet "answering" the other in an agreed-upon form.
- Rewriting each other's poems or adding to each other's poems.
- Intermingling your own poetic lines with those of a poet you admire.
- Writing with a group of four to ten other writers for a set number of hours with previously agreed-upon rules. For instance, six writers agree to write a series of four-line stanzas, taking turns passing a big notebook around, on the subject of war; or, a certain number of writers get together for one or two hours and write a series of interlocking poems about the seasons. You can make your own rules.
- In prose: two writers writing alternating chapters of a novel, or two writers interviewing each other.

As you can see, there are limitless possibilities for the collaboration, which is an experiment conducted to find out what we can discover about poetry by working with others that we could not discover on our own. The old saying reminds us: "Two heads are better than one." As poets we often write about ourselves, the "I" from which we learn about the world. To understand more about ourselves and about writing, it is fascinating and useful to collaborate with other writers. What we mean by the poet's "inspiration" is often the introduction of startling and surprising words and ideas into the poem — in collaborative work these surprises happen often.

A poet who in this century helped write a linked poem in the tradition of the Japanese *renga* said that poets are like trees, all united by their roots in the earth and their branches in the sky, and that there is a moment when the poetry of all people is alike, and that there is one voice which always says the same thing.

It is important to be oneself and it is also important to be connected or linked with others because that is what creates the usefulness of knowledge. Though the outcomes of collaborations don't "belong" to any one person, they are often good poems and they provide writers and readers with new ideas about writing and the world.

See also: RENGA.

Concrete Poem

Concrete poems use space. They use sound. Instead of simply letting the words stand for something else (the way, for example, the word *leaf* refers to a real, physical leaf), the words in the poem dramatize their meaning by the way they look. They draw attention to their physical appearance, ink on the page. The poem becomes a collage of words, letters, and other symbols that may or may not have something to do with the meaning we usually assign to them. You can do more than use plain words to create the visual effect of the concrete poem. You can use different typefaces, colors, and symbols, all in the hope of making the poem not only something you read but something you see. Thus, in one kind of concrete poem, verbs might act themselves out and nouns might take on the shape and color of what they mean.

```
        W a t c h i n g
              w a i t i n g  w e
!!!!!!!!!!!!!!YELL!!!!!!!!!!!!!!
        when    we    see
-----------
            see
            the
            f
             a
              l
           l
            i
           n
            g
              leaf
    that lands on the ground

    gets c s                    marching f
      rushedhedd   c u  p ed by marching e
                  r  m l        marching e
                    o                    t
                  l  w
    and then is b    n

                    away
```

52

Concrete poems have literary ancestors in what are called "shaped poems." The seventeenth-century English poet George Herbert wrote poems that took on the shape of the subject of the poem (for example, the poem "Easter Wings" looks like a pair of wings on the page). Guillaume Apollinaire, a French poet in the early part of the twentieth century, created a variation on shaped poems called calligrams; these poems also took on the shape of the things he was writing about (a heart, a mirror, or a carnation).

Since the 1950s, poets who have explored concrete poetry include Emmett Williams, Ian Hamilton Finlay, Haroldo de Campos, Edwin Morgan, and Mathias Goeritz. In their poems, they see poetry as a visual or graphic art. They see it as something that can be abstract and that must be looked at in order to be understood. In trying to enhance the meaning of the poem, as well as to free the poem from what these poets see as its linguistic or verbal limitations, they have made typeface, symbol, shape, and the spatial relationships between letters, words, and lines fundamental elements of composition.

In the following examples, the poets have explored how a poem's look affects its impact. In the first, by Roger McGough, we note how the title of the poem, which refers to middle-aged love, also refers to a tennis match, thus linking middle-aged love to that match. The reader's eye moves back and forth across the net, watching, in effect, the competition.

40 -------------------- Love

middle	aged
couple	playing
ten	nis
when	the
game	ends
and	they
go	home
the	net
will	still
be	be-
tween	them

53

like   attracts   like

like   attracts   like

like   attracts   like

like   attracts   like

like   attracts   like

like   attracts like

like attracts like

likeattractslike

likeattractslike

likeattractlike

likattraclike

likttralike

liktelikts

— Emmett Williams

Figure 3

silencio silencio silencio
silencio silencio silencio
silencio   silencio
silencio silencio silencio
silencio silencio silencio

—Eugen Gomringer

Figure 4

In the Emmett Williams poem (figure 3), the two words "like," which are the same, move closer and closer to each other, thus making the meaning of the poem come true.

In the final example (figure 4), by Eugen Gomringer, the word *silencio* (silence) is used to build a wall, which, with the center word removed, creates a stillness, a space by which silence may be heard.

There are a lot of ways to write concrete poems. One way is to make the poem abstract, as Gomringer does with his poem, making the poem's appearance mean everything. Another way to write a concrete poem is to come up with a topic (a house and its rooms, the beach, people talking or playing or fighting) and then try to make the appearance of the words reflect what they mean (for example, in the first poem above, the way the word "falling" actually falls down the page). You can highlight all this by using colors ("leaf" could be green or red and brown), or by varying the typeface to represent the different ways you want the words to be emphasized. You can find different typefaces for words in magazines and newspapers. Depending on the size and style, these can represent a variety of ideas about what the words and the poem will grow to mean.

See also: CALLIGRAM.

Couplet
("CUP-let")

The couplet is a couple, or pair, of lines of poetry, usually rhymed. The word *couplet* comes from the French, and in England the couplet developed when the French controlled that country (1066-1350).

There are different types of couplets and different ways of making couplets work. In the *iambic pentameter couplet*, first used by Geoffrey Chaucer, each line has ten syllables, alternating unaccented and accented; Chaucer varied this pattern quite a bit. Later writers — such as John Dryden and Alexander Pope — made good use of the iambic pentameter couplet (also called "heroic couplets").

Couplets can be either closed or open. In the *closed couplet,* the thought or image is neatly packaged in the two lines, as in Pope's

> Know, nature's children all divide her care;
> The fur that warms a monarch, warmed a bear.

In the *open couplet,* the second line of the couplet runs right into the next couplet, as in this excerpt from John Milton's "L'Allegro":

> And ever against eating cares
> Lap me in soft Lydian airs
> Married to immortal verse
> Such as the meeting soul may pierce
> In notes with many a winding bout
> Of linked sweetness long drawn out.

The technique of running one line over into the next is called *enjambment.* Enjambment keeps couplets from becoming too predictable and singsongy, as they do when they come to a stop at the end of each line (or, as we say, they are *endstopped*). Another way of varying the rhythmic flow of the lines is to have pauses somewhere in the middle of the lines; these pauses are called *caesuras.*

57

Not all couplets are of the heroic type. Some have shorter lines, others longer ones. Jonathan Swift was a master of a shorter-lined couplet that has only four beats per line, as in his spoof, "A Satyrical Elegy on the Death of a Late Famous General":

And could he be indeed so old
As by the news-papers we're told?
Threescore, I think, is pretty high;
'Twas time in conscience he should die.
This world he cumber'd long enough;
He burnt his candle to the snuff;
And that's the reason some folks think,
He left behind *so great a stink*."

Sometimes the couplet stands alone as a two-line poem, as in this one by Robert Frost:

The Span of Life

The old dog barks backwards without getting up.
I can remember when he was a pup.

Short poems such as this pack a lot of punch into a little space by making a simple description in the first line, pausing between lines to let it sink in, and then adding a second line that makes us go back and think again about the first line. It makes us realize that the poem's message is larger than it might have seemed at first. In delivering a brief but potent message, the couplet is like an epigram.

The couplet also serves as a summary or pithy pronouncement at the end of a longer poem, such as a sonnet. Shakespeare's "Sonnet 18" talks about how poetry can confer a kind of immortality on mortals:

So long as men can breathe or eyes can see
So long lives this and this gives life to thee.

Basically, by having two equal parts, the couplet is a simple and fundamental structure that reflects so many other basic structures in and around us, such as the human body's two eyes, two ears, two hands, and so on, as well as our thought patterns of yes/no, up/down, and good/bad. It is not surprising that such patterns are reflected in the way we speak, and can be used consciously for great effect, as in John Kennedy's inaugural address:

Ask not what your country can do for you.
Ask what you can do for your country.

See also: FOOT, LINE, EPIGRAM, and SONNET.

Eclogue
("ECK-log")

The word *eclogue* comes from the ancient Greek, meaning "select pieces." Eclogues (also called "bucolics") are poems written in the form of a monologue or dialogue in which the speaker tells us what he or she feels about a particular theme, why he or she feels that way, and why he or she believes others ought to feel the same. Usually the writing is smooth and flowing, the setting pastoral (that is, in a country setting).

The first writer of eclogues is thought to be Theocritus, a Greek poet writing around 300 B.C. Theocritus wrote twenty-eight eclogues whose style and subject matter, from life in the country to the relationships between the gods and men, have been models for other eclogue writers ever since.

The Roman poet Virgil is generally considered to be the finest and most innovative of eclogue writers. Inspired by Theocritus, Virgil's eclogues cover such themes as the romance of shepherds, poetry contests, and the adventures of Silenus with two shepherds.

Virgil's eclogues, however, are more diverse in both form and content. Lyrical and full of imagery, his eclogues also tend to use situation and character dramatically (they were often performed on the stage at theater festivals). Also, they pay keener attention to describing real, as opposed to idealized, rural settings. They use the eclogue as a way to talk about philosophical and political matters (one eclogue discusses land distribution, others have as characters political exiles who talk about the conditions of their lives). With Virgil the eclogue is no longer a decorative, narrative form but rather a poetic form for considering the ideas and actions of individuals and groups within contemporary society.

Since then, some of the eclogue's characteristic features have changed. It has ceased to be defined strictly as a pastoral. It now has whatever setting the poet desires, depending on the point to be made. A country setting means the poet wants to talk about the virtues of a simple, natural life. A city setting means the poet wants to talk about progress and its effects on daily life. The eclogue is not a very popular form anymore; its talky, instructive qualities don't seem to appeal to people now. In the twentieth century, few poets have been interested in working with the form (Robert Frost is a notable exception).

To write an eclogue, start with a topic or theme you'd like to explore. Give it a setting and characters that reflect or contrast with your message and that will add dramatic effect. If you are going to use one speaker, you'll want the speaker to focus clearly on the advantages of his or her point of view and to contrast them effectively with the disadvantages of the opposite. If you are using more than one speaker, the structure and development of ideas will be a little more complicated. If the speakers agree, each can add to and develop points made by the other. If the speakers disagree, you'll have to allow each to develop his/her point of view before finally having one side come out the "winner." Remember that the strength of the eclogue depends on how convincing it is, how strongly, through images and argument, you can make your point.

See also: PASTORAL POEM.

Elegy
("EL-uh-gee")

The elegy is one of the oldest poetic forms, going back at least to the ancient Greeks, when it was written to express the sadness of a death. The word *elegy* comes from the Greek word *elegeia,* which means "song of mourning," and these poems were popular in the Greek tragedies.

While there is such a thing as an elegiac stanza — a fairly structured four-line stanza written in iambic pentameter and rhymed *abab* — the elegy itself has no given form. A poem is called an elegy because of what it says, not how it says it. However, a loose structure or pattern can be seen in the classical elegies of the Greeks. Classical elegies start out with a statement of the subject (usually a specific death), followed by the lamentations or mourning of this death, and finally consolation, as the poet came to accept the loss.

The first person to write an elegy was probably Mimnermus of Colophon, a Greek who lived in the seventh century B.C. It's hard to be sure that he wrote the first one, because it is so long ago, but there are fragments still existing from his two books of elegies. In his poems, he wrote about how wonderful it was to be young and alive, and how horrible the thought of death was to him.

Among the Romans in the first century B.C., love chased death from the elegy, and the elegy became instead the preferred poetic form for love poetry. Tibullus, Propertius, and Ovid were the three principal Latin love elegists. This Latin influence was felt in France in the 1500s, when Clément Marot published the first book of love elegies in French. The French poets, Pierre de Ronsard and Louise Labé also wrote love elegies during this same period.

Elegies have been written throughout the ages in many countries, including Italy, Germany, Spain, France, and England. It was in England in 1611 that the connection between the elegy and death was reintroduced with Donne's use of a funeral elegy. This idea of elegy as a lament for the dead was picked up by the German poets Goethe and Schiller.

Then in 1750, the English poet Thomas Gray wrote his well-known poem, "Elegy Written in a Country Churchyard." It wasn't about any particular death, but rather Gray's thoughts and feelings while sitting among the graves. Toward the end of the poem, he imagines the death of a man and the poem ends with this epitaph, "He gave to Misery all he had — a tear; He gain'd from Heaven ('twas all he wish'd) a Friend." Other well-known English elegies are Milton's "Lycidas" and Shelley's "Adonais."

Another famous writer of the elegy was Rainer Maria Rilke, a German poet. In 1912, he began a series of ten poems called the "Duino Elegies," written in a castle at Duino, in Austria. The poems are about art and death and how humans struggle with both these ideas. Another modern elegy is Federico Garcia Lorca's "Lament for Ignacio Sánchez Mejías."

A good example of an elegy is Walt Whitman's "When Lilacs Last in the Dooryard Bloom'd." He wrote this poem in 1865, shortly after the Civil War. Whitman served as a nurse during the war and saw many young soldiers die. The poem shows Whitman finally accepting the nation's loss and his own, the death of Abraham Lincoln and the death of the soldiers. By the end of the poem he sees death's place in the natural cycle of life. It's a long poem, written in sixteen sections. Here are the first two sections:

1

When lilacs last in the dooryard bloom'd,
And the great star early droop'd in the western sky in the night,
I mourn'd, and yet shall mourn with ever-returning spring.

Ever-returning spring, trinity sure to me you bring,
Lilac blooming perennial and drooping star in the west,
And thought of him I love.

2

O powerful western fallen star!
O shades of night — O moody, tearful night!
O great star disappear'd — O the black murk that hides the star!
O cruel hands that hold me powerless — O helpless soul of me!
O harsh surrounding cloud that will not free my soul.

Throughout the poem Whitman never names the people he is mourning, but he compares their death to a star disappearing into the black sky of night and he compares his grief to a harsh surrounding cloud.

In its broadest sense, an elegy is a poem about something ending: either love or life or a moment. Try to write a poem about something that has ended for you. The poem could be about a person you love who has died, or it could be about the end of a day. In this poem, show how you feel by comparing this ending to other endings, the way Whitman does.

See also: EPITAPH.

Epic
("EH-pick")

Epic (from the Greek *epos*, a speech, story, or song) literally means to speak or to tell a tale. The epic is a very long narrative (story) poem that tells of the adventures of a hero. Homer's *Iliad* and *Odyssey*, Virgil's *Aeneid*, and Dante's *Divine Comedy* are famous examples of epic poetry.

Homer's books are based on stories of the Trojan War that are thought to have been told and retold for many years before they were written down. Virgil's *Aeneid* is an extension of Homer's story, and Virgil himself appears as a character in Dante's poem.

Epics serve the purpose of enabling their audiences to understand the past and to control their own destiny through the inspiration of the poem's noble ideals. The epic poem is meant to enhance the reader's sense of good and evil. Epics most often focus on the heroism of one person who exists as a symbol of strength, virtue, and courage in the face of conflict.

The traditional epic is divided into a series of books or cantos. Many of the epics of the past were written in the poetic meter called dactylic (from the Greek *dactylos*, meaning the three joints of a finger) hexameter. This means that each line contains six metrical feet of three beats each, the first a long syllable and the second and third short syllables.

An epic must be able to tell a tale in poetry about heroism that can be retained in the reader's memory, or retell stories that everyone already knows, such as myths or historical events. Though *Moby Dick* by Herman Melville and the American Indian trickster/coyote tales are epic in nature, they are not written in the epic form. Some works are called "epic" just because they're long.

The type of epic that is comic in nature (such as Byron's *Don Juan*) is called the "mock epic."

Long modern poems that can be construed as being epics are Walt Whitman's *Leaves of Grass* (a book of poems about America in the nineteenth century in which the author himself becomes the hero), William Carlos Williams' *Paterson* (a historical book in prose and poetry about Paterson, New Jersey), Stephen Vincent Benét's *John Brown's Body* (a long poem about the Civil War), and Buckminster Fuller's *Epic on the History of Industrialization*.

Subjects for a modern epic could include Martin Luther King, spaceflight, the history of native Americans, Mahatma Gandhi, Malcolm X, Carl Sagan, the history of modern physics, Jerry Lewis, the Vietnam War, the Cold War, and one day in the life of a person.

It is important to remember, when writing an epic poem, that it is not a biography of the hero or heroine, nor does it give a whole history of the subject, but begins in the middle of things and tells the story of one important year or some shorter span of time, in order to inspire the readers to be good and true.

See also: CANTO, OTTAVA RIMA, TERZA RIMA.

Epigram
("EP-ih-gram")

An epigram (from the Greek *epigramma*, to write upon) is a short, witty poem or saying that is easy to remember and is written to be remembered. A popular example of an epigram is: "Experience is the name everyone gives to his or her mistakes." In the past, epigrams were often inscriptions carved on monuments, tombstones, and statues.

Epigrams have no particular form except their brevity (two, four or six lines) and their way of getting right to the point. They can be written to compliment or insult another person, to make a political point, to praise or ridicule a hero, to make a sudden and shocking statement about love, to make a dedication, to give advice, to make fun of life, to commemorate a dead person, to express a philosophy of life, and to send a secret message that is hidden behind the obvious meanings of the words. Another interesting epigrammatic form involves the poet pretending to be an inanimate object, like a ship or a stone, and writing in the first person as that thing. Epigrams like these are sometimes also riddles.

The Greek Anthology is an ancient collection of more than 1,500 epigrams of all kinds. Here are two examples from *The Greek Anthology* about love:

> Love made it grow and sharpened it, Heliodora's fingernail,
> Now her scratching reaches to my heart
> — *Meleager*

> We're right to call love a three-time loser—
> Love wakes us up, love is reckless, and then
> love strips us bare
> — *Diophanes*

Here is one written by an anonymous poet about the death of the Greek playwright Sophocles:

> Your light's out now, old Sophocles, flower of poets
> Crowned with Bacchus's purple grapes

Some popular epigrams written in English are:

> Sir, I admit your general rule,
> That every poet is a fool:
> But you yourself may serve to show it,
> That every fool is not a poet.
> —*Alexander Pope*

> You are a poet
> But you don't know it
> But your feet show it
> Because they're Longfellows.
> —*Anonymous*

> *Miss Bernadette is so white*
> *They mark her absent in the morning*
> —*Anonymous, P.S. 154, New York*

Epigrams have a lot to do with what makes all of us human: a sense of humor and a desire for immortality. The English poet John Dryden wrote this epigram as a joke:

> Here lies my wife: here let her lie!
> Now she's at rest, and so am I.

Because the epigram is a poetic form, it can be used to insult another person with grace and humor, for example:

> A lawyer thinks he is always right
> Just like Moises Gomez.
> —*Eric Melendez, P.S. 154, New York*

> My Friend, if you want to be cruel,
> Breathe on Russia.
> —*Moises Gomez, P.S. 154, New York*

Epigrams are similar to what we might say to each other in witty conversation about the events of the day, with the difference that the epigram is written on paper or cut in stone to last forever.

See also: EPITAPH.

Epistle
("e-PISS-ul")

Epistola is the Latin word for *letter.* An epistle is a poem that is also a letter. There is no single form for the verse epistle.

The Latin poet Horace wrote perhaps the most famous verse epistles. His epistles use plain language to discuss literary, moral, and philosophical ideas and to gossip about people he knew, giving us a pretty good idea of how he and his friends lived and what they valued.

Today, because the most common type of letter is the business letter, we expect letters to be somewhat formal. But before the invention of the telephone, people often wrote letters with the same kind of friendly, informal tone that they use talking on the telephone (some still do). Like any letter, the tone and substance of an epistle will depend on the person it is directed to. If you are writing to a senator or to a prospective employer, your tone will be much more formal than if you are writing to a pal.

Epistles can be several pages long (like the famous "Epistle to Dr. Arbuthnot" of Alexander Pope) or they can be as short as a postcard.

> Dear Joanne,
>
> Last night Magda dreamed that she,
> you, Jack, and I were driving around
> Italy.
>
> We parked in Florence and left
> our dog to guard the car.
>
> She was worried because he
> doesn't understand Italian.
>
> Lew

This little epistle was written to a real person by another real person, Lew Welch. But you could also write an epistle that wasn't from you but from someone you invented and to anybody you like. The following letter is signed with the name Joe and is addressed to Joe's mother, but it was written by the poet Langston Hughes.

Dear Mama,

    Time I pay rent and get my food
and laundry I don't have much left
but here is five dollars for you
to show you I still appreciates you.
My girl-friend send her love and say
she hopes to lay eyes on you sometime in life.
Mama, it has been raining cats and dogs up
here. Well, that is all so I will close.

Your son baby,
Respectably as ever,
Joe

Poems are where anything you want to happen can, so you don't have to limit yourself to letters you might normally write. You can also write epistles to a grandmother who died, to your dog or cat, to a cactus, a cloud, or a baseball glove. The trick is just to keep in mind who or what you are writing to and what they might be interested in.

Epitaph
("EP-ih-taff")

An epitaph (from Greek, meaning "upon a tomb") is an inscription on a tomb, or writing suitable for that purpose.

The epitaph can be in prose or poetry; if poetry, it can be in any rhythmical pattern or none, rhymed or unrhymed. It should not be confused with the elegy, which, although often similar to the epitaph in subject and tone, is quite a bit longer.

Epitaphs range from the lofty to the coarse, from the sublimely serious to the shockingly hilarious. Some people have used satire to write their enemy's epitaph long *before* the enemy died.

The earliest examples of epitaphs, carved in stone, are from ancient Egypt. The Greeks and Romans became conscious of the epitaph as a literary form. Elegies were written throughout the Middle Ages, too, but it wasn't until the 15th century in England that the epitaph developed into an exceptionally high art.

Here are some examples of epitaphs.

> Underneath this sod lies John Round,
> Who was lost at sea, and never was found.

For a girl dead at seventeen:

> Sleep soft in dust until the Almighty will,
> Then rise, unchanged, and be an angel still.

*

> Here lies I
> Killed by a sky
> Rocket in my eye.

The following prose epitaph was written to commemorate a man who was scalded to death: "Sacred to the memory of our 'steamed friend." Most epitaphs, however, are sober and serious:

Epitaph on Elizabeth, L.H.

Wouldst thou hear what man can say
  In a little? Reader, stay.
Underneath this stone doth lie
  As much beauty as could die;
Which in life did harbor give
  To more virtue than doth live.
If at all she had a fault,
  Leave it buried in this vault.
One name was Elizabeth,
  Th' other let it sleep with death;
Fitter, where it died to tell,
  Than that it lived at all. Farewell.
      —*Ben Jonson*

See also: ELEGY, EPIGRAM.

Epithalamium
("ep-ih-thah-LAME-ee-oom")

The epithalamium is also called *epithalamion* and comes from a Greek word meaning "upon the bridal chamber." The epithalamium is a poem that celebrates a marriage.

Although there is no single fixed form for epithalamiums, they all have certain features: their subject is a particular marriage, they tell something about the wedding day, they praise the bride and groom, sometimes they tell about the bride and groom's past, they give blessings for the marriage and good wishes for its future happiness. Because the poet has lots of nice things to say about the bride and groom, and lots of blessings and good wishes to bestow, the epithalamium is not a short poem. It usually runs from around 40 to 400 lines. Some epithalamiums use rhyme and meter, others don't.

Traditional marriage songs have existed in most cultures, but the Greek poet Sappho, who lived around 600 B.C., is credited with having made the epithalamium a distinct literary form. In ancient times the epithalamium was sung by a chorus of boys and girls right outside the honeymooners' bedroom!

The Greeks and Romans wrote many epithalamiums, and the form was widely used in England, France, and Italy during the Renaissance. The first epithalamium in English was by Sir Philip Sidney, celebrating his own wedding (1580). Other notable examples are Edmund Spenser's "Epithalamium," John Donne's "Epithalamium Made at Lincoln's Inn," Robert Herrick's "An Epithalamie to Sir Thomas Southwell and his Ladie," Andrew Marvell's "Two Songs at the Marriage of the Lord Fauconberg and the Lady Mary Cromwell," Percy Shelley's "Fragment: Supposed to Be an Epithalamium of Francis Ravaillac and Charlotte Corday," and Alfred, Lord Tennyson's "To H.R.H. Princess Beatrice." Well-known twentieth-century examples are Guillaume Apollinaire's "Poem

Read at the Wedding of André Salmon," and Frank O'Hara's "Poem Read at Joan Mitchell's."

If people you know are getting married and you want to give them something special, why not write them an epithalamium?

Event Poem

Event poems emerged in the late 1950s, the same time as the art form called "Happenings." In fact, an event poem could be seen as the written equivalent of a Happening. A Happening is a dramatic presentation that might use performers, sound, lights, costumes, props, and music. But unlike a play, Happenings have no stage or "story." Instead, strange and unpredictable things happen, some by plan, some by chance, sometimes among the spectators.

Here is the text for a Happening that never happened, by Allan Kaprow, one of the best-known Happening artists:

> Naked women eat giant bowls of Cheerios and milk atop a
> mountain of used tires. Children disgorge barrels of
> whitewash over the mountain. A hundred yards away, men and
> women swimmers in brightly colored plastic pools continually
> leap out of the water to catch with their mouths rubber
> gaskets festooned with Life Saver candies that hang from
> chains of men's belts. The mountain is taken down, tire by
> tire, and moved into the pools, and the water spills out. The
> children tie the adults together with the belts. They pour
> whitewash over the now still heaps of bodies. Then they
> buckle dozens more of the belts around their necks, waists,
> and legs. They take the remaining Life Savers to a
> factory-fresh tire shop and offer them for sale in laughy
> voices.

To create an Event Poem, select an object, a pineapple, say. Since a pineapple's *ordinary* uses are involved with eating, drinking the juice, putting it on the table as a decoration, or cutting off the leafy end and planting it, you will not do any of these. Instead, you will find new, imaginative (sometimes slightly crazy) uses for it. Number these and write them down, each below the other, beginning each sentence with an *action* verb: put, pretend, kick, cut, chew, look, etc. For example:

1. Cut the leaves off a pineapple and use it as a football to throw a touchdown pass.
2. Hollow out the pineapple, fill it with pebbles, shake it like a maraca and create reggae music.
3. Pluck out ten leaves, polish them, and wear them as fingernails to a Halloween party.

After three or four imaginative uses of the pineapple, you might move on to the way it looks. One poet wrote a whole poem about simply looking imaginatively at a pineapple. He thought it looked like a green genie coming out of a bottle, like yesterday's volcano, like a green sea washing up over a high rock.

The third part of an event poem might have to do with touch: "Feel the pineapple. It feels like a cat's claws scratching my hand."

Here is an example of a complete Pineapple Event poem by a student.

Pineapple Event Poem

1. Cut the pineapple in half and wear the two halves as earmuffs on a cold winter day.
2. Peel the skins off 100 pineapples and glue them down to the floor as tiles.
3. Cut out five of the little round lozenges on the pineapple skin and sew them on your jacket as buttons.
4. Look at the pineapple. It looks like the torch of the Statue of Liberty.
5. Feel the pineapple. It feels like a suede sneaker on the foot of a very large kid.

To create your own event poem, choose an *object* — peanut butter, an ice cube, a banana, a hairbrush, spaghetti, a cotton ball, are just a few possibilities — and think of other uses for it besides the ordinary ones. Number these, as in the pineapple event poem, and start each sentence with a verb. Write at least three uses, then move on to looking at the object and finally to touching it. Or, if you want, mix them all up.

See also: PERFORMANCE POEM.

Foot

Say the word *create* aloud. Notice that you say it "cre-ATE" (not "CRE-ate"). The first syllable is unaccented, the second accented. An unaccented syllable, followed by an accented one, is an example of one kind of poetic "foot" (the one called the "iamb"). So, the word *create* is iambic. As you'll see below, there are other kinds of poetic feet (or "measures").

Now say aloud this line: "I walked across the world to kiss your hand." Notice that this line is composed of iambic feet, five of them: "I walked | across | the world | to kiss | your hand." When a line of poetry has a regular rhythmic pattern, as this one does, we say it is in a particular *meter*. The meter of this example is called "iambic pentameter." This means that there are five feet of iambic meter [- /] in every line. (The hyphen stands for an unaccented syllable; the slash mark for an accented syllable.)

The names of our meters come from ancient Greek poetry. The most common meters in English are:

• **Iamb** ("EYE-amb"): One unaccented syllable followed by one accented long syllable: - /. Oddly enough, this powerful and dignified rhythm in English and American poetry was originally used in Greek poetry (and called the *iambos*, from the verb *iambiazo* — "to assail in iambics" or "to lampoon") to make fun of a victim or to insult him. It is justly famous as the meter of Shakespeare's plays:

FEET	1	2	3	4	5
IAMBIC METER	-/	-/	-/	-/	-/

In Example 1 below, from John Milton's sonnet "On His Blindness," the line of iambic pentameter is "regular"; each foot is a perfect iamb:

Example 1:   _ / - / - / - / - /
(regular)   When I consider how my light is spent

79

Example 2 — the first line of Hamlet's famous soliloquy —

Example 2: _ / _ / _ / / _ _ / _
(irregular) To be or not to be, that is the question

is "irregular" in that it contains eleven syllables rather than ten. Also, the fourth and fifth feet are not iambic. We know this because it would be silly to say here "that IS the QUEStion" rather than the more natural-sounding "THAT is the QUEStion."

The lesson here is that poets do not set up a rhythm and follow it rigidly, without variations. Be prepared to find poets "breaking the rules," even their own rules, all over the place. Especially great poets.

• **Trochee** ("TROW-key"): One accented syllable followed by one unaccented syllable — the opposite of the iamb: / - . *Trochee* comes from the Greek verb *trekho*, "run," which also gives us *track* and *trek* in English. The Greeks believed that the trochee moved faster than the more stately iamb — it was a "running" foot.

Example: / _ / _ / _ / _ / _
Don't you ever oversleep on Monday?

• **Dactyl** ("DACK-till"): One accented syllable followed by two unaccented syllables: / - - . In Greek, *daktulos* meant "finger," and looking at your finger will remind you of its structure: a finger is made up of one long bone and two shorter bones. Here is a famous example, the first line of Henry Wadsworth Longfellow's poem, *Evangeline:*

Example: / _ _ / _ _ / _ _ / _ _ / _ _ / _
This is the forest primeval. The murmuring pines and the hemlocks

• **Anapest** ("AN-uh-pest"): Two unaccented syllables followed by one accented syllable, the opposite of the dactyl: - - / . *Anapest* comes from two Greek words, *ana* ("up") and the verb *paio* ("to strike" or "hit"). The anapest moves "up" or "toward" the "struck" or accented syllable: sha-da-BOOM.

Example: _ _ / _ _ / _ _ / _ _ /
By a hole in the woods sat a green little boy

Example: _ _ / _ _ / _ _ / _ _ /
Architectural plans have a right to be blue

• **Spondee** ("SPON-dee"): Two accented syllables: / / . *Spondee* comes from the Greek word for a libation (a ceremonial pouring of wine). The music accompanying such libations was usually slow and solemn, for these libations were done to celebrate important occasions. In the first line below (from Thomas Hardy's poem "The Garden Seat"), the spondee is "break down":

Example: Soon it will break down unaware

Example: Bad heart, flat feet, sad shoes — bad news.

You don't have to know these technical terms to write a poem, any more than you have to know what a half note is to make up a song. The truth is that many contemporary poets, some of them quite good, have a hard time keeping these technical terms straight. The terms do provide the vocabulary for talking about what you see in a poem's rhythms when you examine them closely and thoroughly.

See also: LINE, RHYTHM.

Found Poem

A "found poem" is a piece of writing that was not intended as a poem, but is so declared by its "finder." Parts of newspaper articles are often declared to be "found poems," as are lists, notes passed among children, scraps of conversation, and other incidental uses of language. The closer the original intent of the language comes to that of poetry, the less likely it is to qualify as true found poetry. The odd thing is how the found words seem to take on an added power when removed from their original context and presented alone.

"Writing" a found poem requires simply that you stay alert to those exceptional uses of language or sharply presented, telegraphic stories that create a poetic effect or an emotional response as strong as that made by a poem. The effect or response may or may not have been intended, but the notion of the language as "poetry" must not have played a factor in its creation.

Writing a found poem often requires creative skills similar to those used in the actual creation of the art, deciding the poem's limits and line-breaks. The poet does not enjoy the license to change, add or omit words, a rule often broken.

Dear Mom

Dear Mom,
I ate all my lunch
And went back to school.
I am all washed up.

Here, the poet has simply decided where to break the lines of a brief note found taped to the refrigerator, and capitalized the first letter of each line. In the following short poem, the author is simply quoting his four-year-old son.

Ben Carries the Cracked Egg

This one's for you Geof
I think they'll lay my egg tomorrow

82

The next two poems come from newspaper articles.

The Story of White Man Leading Viet Cong Patrol
— AP Dispatch, Des Moines *Register*, August 4, 1968

The slain enemy resembled
an American Marine
who was 18 years old
when he disappeared.

The violent episode
was one of the strangest
in this strange war.

        *

For a moment
the two young men —
the American Marine
and the white man
in the uniform of the enemy —
stared at each other.

"He had an AK 47
automatic rifle
but he just looked at me."

Gordon fired
after a moment's hesitation.

        *

Several of the Marines suspect
that the unknown white man
whom they call "the Caucasian"
could have shot first
but deliberately held fire.

At the debriefing
everyone was afraid
to say what they had seen.
            — Eric Torgersen

Astronaut Jim Lovell
flying in Gemini 7
high over Hawaii,
today spotted
a tiny pinpoint
of greenish-blue brilliance
far below.
He successfully "locked on"
for 40 seconds
and sent
the world's first communication
down a laser beam
to earth.

"I've got it," Lovell cried.
      —John Giorno

Some of the earliest and most engrossing found poetry is by
Charles Reznikoff in his *Testimony*, based on law reports.

Free Verse

Free verse is just that — lines of poetry that are written without rules: no regular beat and no rhyme. The *vers libre* (French for "free verse") movement began in late nineteenth-century Europe, especially in France. But unrhymed poetry without a regular rhythm had appeared in translations of the Bible, and one of the first great poets to use the form was Walt Whitman, an American.

Whitman thought that American poetry should be free of European influence. His collection of poems, *Leaves of Grass* (1855), is America's great poetic Declaration of Independence. All of it is in free verse. Here is an excerpt from the long poem that came to be called "Song of Myself."

> I believe a leaf of grass is no less than the journeywork of the stars,
> And the pismire is equally perfect, and a grain of sand, and the
>   egg of the wren,
> And the tree-toad is a chef-d'oeuvre for the highest,
> And the running blackberry would adorn the parlors of heaven,
> And the narrowest hinge in my hand puts to scorn all machinery,
> And the cow crunching with depressed head surpasses any statue,
> And a mouse is miracle enough to stagger sextillions of infidels,
> And I could come every afternoon of my life to look at the
>   farmer's girl boiling her iron teakettle and baking shortcake.

The point of free verse is not that it has thrown the traditional rules of poetry out of the window; it means that every poet who writes in this form must work to create his or her *own* rules. These rules are based on our personal thought patterns, our breath patterns, our sense of how the poem should *look* on the page, our deepest feelings about life itself. Free verse grants us the freedom to find our own rhythm, our own heartbeat, rather than traditional rhymed-and-metered poetry, which insists that we follow the patterns laid down by others. No wonder Whitman saw it as a perfect expression of democracy. As his contemporary, the philosopher-poet Henry David Thoreau, wrote: "If a man does not keep pace with his companions, perhaps it is because he hears a different drummer. Let him step to the music which he hears, however measured or far away." Free verse is the "different drummer" of modern poetry. In free verse the *line* is very important. Lines can be long or short, or long and short in the same poem. With free verse, what we must ask ourselves is whether or not the line *looks* and *feels* and *sounds* right. The form (or shape) of the poem that is coming into being as we write it is telling us to watch and listen to it.

So, free verse offers no excuse for sloppy writing. In fact, it demands more of the poet, because he or she must question every word, test the shape and sound of every line, and be able to defend the choices made.

It might be best to begin writing free verse by imitating poets who do it best. Whitman provides an inspiring model in his greatest poems. If Whitman's line is too long for you, look at the tiny free verse poems of Robert Creeley in his collection *For Love*. Creeley's line is very short. William Carlos Williams also wrote brilliantly in the free verse form. Other major poets whose work may be examined to get a feeling for free verse are Theodore Roethke, Kenneth Koch, Frank O'Hara, Allen Ginsberg, John Ashbery, Sylvia Plath, Diane Wakoski, and H.D. (Hilda Doolittle), not to mention the great poets who have written free verse in other languages. By reading these and other poets, you will begin to get a sense of what you want in your own free verse line.

Another approach: write your poem as a paragraph of prose. Then go back and break it up into lines. Do several versions of the poem, one with long lines, one with short lines, and so forth, until the right (for you) shape of the poem begins to emerge. As you do this, you will undoubtedly change things in the poem itself, adding words or descriptions, taking others out. When you feel that you can do no more — like a sculptor who can't cut deeper into the image without ruining it — your poem may be finished.

See also: PROJECTIVE VERSE.

Ghazal
("gah-ZAHL")

The ghazal is a Persian poetry form that takes its name from the Arabic word meaning "the talk of boys and girls," in other words, flirting or sweet talk. The original Persian form was fairly simple—a poem of five to twelve couplets (two-line stanzas), all using the same rhyme, with the poet putting his name in the final stanza.

The ghazal became very popular as a poetry form in Persia around A.D. 1000. Some of the reasons for its popularity were that it was easy to sing and, because it was a relatively short poem, it was easier to write and to hear than a longer poem.

Hundreds of Persian poets, including Sanai, Hafiz, Rumi, and Jami, wrote in this style, which continues to be popular to the present day. But the golden age of the ghazal was between 1100 and 1500. Originally the main themes of the ghazal were love and drinking wine, but later poets became more philosophical and even mystical in their writings.

Ralph Waldo Emerson, the American poet and philosopher, criticized the form of the ghazal, saying the individual lines were like the unstrung beads of a necklace, that there was little unity in these poems. In a sense he was right, as one of the characteristics of the line of a ghazal is that it can stand on its own and be understood, almost like a proverb or saying.

However, if you look at a ghazal like a piece of music where each line adds something to the whole thought, rather than like a story that needs to make sense, then you can begin to understand how the poem hangs together. The unity of a ghazal is based on the idea of a theme and its variations.

The form became known in Europe when *The Divan of Muhammed Shemsed Din Hafiz* was translated into German in 1812. *Divan* means a collection of poems and Hafiz was a famous Persian poet who wrote in the thirteenth century. Hafiz wrote about the joy of living. The German poet Goethe felt a great affinity to Hafiz and copied this form, writing his own collection called *The West-Eastern Divan.* The American poet Robert Bly has translated Rumi's ghazals in a book called *Night & Sleep.*

In its contemporary form, the ghazal doesn't usually rhyme, poets don't sign their name in the last couplet, and it isn't very often about love or drinking. So you might wonder what's left of the original Persian form.

The two important features of the contemporary ghazal are the long-lined couplets (sometimes unrhymed) and the often mystical thoughts that are expressed. Here is an example of a modern-day ghazal:

A Ghazal

There's an inside of me and an outside of me.
The clouds block the sky and the grass has dried golden.

Only a fool would try to love when the heart's in the wrong
    place.
The tree is trying to tell me something but I'm deaf with longing.

Take away my pen, my paper, the table and I am only
a woman, crouched over air, thinking.

My bed sags in the middle and my dreams get caught in my
    throat.
The wind comes in my window but the stars are stuck on the
    screen.

It doesn't take very long to realize you're dead, but alive,
you can go minutes without knowing it. Take a deep breath.

In this ghazal, the poet is sitting at a table trying to write, but at the same time is aware of what's going on around her. She's recording all her thoughts as they come into her mind. These thoughts come out as if they are the truths of the moment.

Try to write a ghazal. Look around you right now, notice where you are and write down some of the truths of what you see and feel. Use the form of the ghazal to structure your thoughts. Two long lines and then a break. If you feel like it, go back to the older Persian form and include your name in the last couplet.

Haiku
("HI-coo")

The haiku is not only a poetic form, but also a genre (type) of poetry. That is, along with its typical form, the haiku has characteristic content and a certain style of language. Of the three — form, content, and language — form is least important.

One expert on the Japanese haiku called it a "poem recording the essence of a moment keenly perceived in which nature is linked to human nature." Haiku poets write about common, everyday experiences, usually involving natural objects. They avoid complicated words and grammar; many haiku don't have complete sentences. Usually haiku have no metaphors or similes. The most common form for haiku is three short lines, the first and third about the same length and the middle one a bit longer, with no rhyme. But the history of haiku includes many variations.

The haiku began many years ago in Japan, where poets used to get together for parties to write long poems, called *renga,* made up of many short stanzas that they took turns writing. Poets going to a renga party hoped that they would have the honor of giving the first stanza, and often made up one or two on the way. Usually only one renga would be written at a party; this meant a lot of "starting verses," or *hokku,* were never used. About five hundred years ago, poets began publishing their unused starting verses in collections, along with the renga they had helped to write. By 1900 the Japanese recognized these detached hokku as fully independent poems, and began calling them "haiku."

Starting verses by master renga poets became models for their students, and have been handed down for generations. English translations of two favorite haiku by the great master Matsuo Bashō (1644-1694) show the range of subject and tone; the first is the best-known poem in Japan:

old pond...   well! let's go
a frog leaps in   snow-viewing till
water's sound   we tumble!

Some have said that the point of the "old pond" poem is the inner peace needed to appreciate such a small event. The second poem speaks of the Japanese custom of going out to look at beautiful things at different seasons, such as the blossoms of flowering trees in the spring, the full moon in autumn, and the snowy fields and mountains of winter. Bashō likes to do this too, and jokingly shows some of the excitement involved. (But notice that he does *not* say anything like "how peaceful it is!" or "Oh, I'm so excited!")

At the beginning of the twentieth century, some American and English poets (including Amy Lowell, Ezra Pound, Wallace Stevens, and William Carlos Williams) used the simplicity and directness of traditional Japanese haiku as examples of the way they wanted to change our poetry. At the same time, some Japanese haiku poets abandoned traditional ideas about what a haiku should talk about and the form it should be written in, because they admired European and American poems.

Today poets write haiku in many languages around the world, each maintaining some essential features of haiku. Here are some examples:

bass
picking bugs
off the moon
      — *Nicholas A. Virgilio*

the sun goes down —
my shovel strikes a spark
from the dark earth
      — *Cor van den Heuvel*

light
up under the gull's wing:
sunrise
      — *Ruth M. Yarrow*

what was I thinking?
toes suddenly cool
in river clay
      — *Rod Willmot*

All these poems have features that make them haiku. In content they all involve nature. Also, the words and expressions in these poems are simple, relating to things directly, without metaphors and similes, and with almost no adjectives. Only two of them have complete sentences.

Some people believe (mistakenly) that a haiku must have seventeen syllables arranged 5/7/5 in lines 1, 2, and 3. The fact is that traditional Japanese haiku poets count "sounds," not syllables. The seventeen sounds of a traditional Japanese haiku take about the same length of time to say as twelve to fifteen English syllables. That's why most North American haiku poets write haiku in English with fewer than seventeen syllables. Today many poets simply write haiku in three short lines.

Finally, city life increasingly finds its way into haiku:

> red light
> gasoline sloshing
> in the tank
> > —André Duhaime
> > Tr. Dorothy Howard

> Soaked
> in morning dew
>
> a parking ticket
> > —Chūsaburō Itō
> > Tr. David Aylward

To write a haiku that sounds traditional, make sure it shows the reader something to look at or hear or smell or taste or touch, and let it have three lines with the first and last a bit shorter than the middle. Do not add words to fill out the pattern. As with any kind of poetry that interests you, read lots of examples by many poets.

See also: RENGA, SENRYU, TANKA.

Imitation

For many centuries, philosphers and writers have discussed how art imitates life and how words imitate things. But in talking about imitations here, we mean a poem that derives from a poem in another language, and yet cannot be called a translation.

The poet Robert Lowell used the word this way in the title of his *Imitations*, a collection of Lowell's poems based on his translations of poems by other poets. The traditional translator tries to make the translation as close an approximation to the original text as possible. Lowell, a poet, found that his translations took on a life of their own, a life that was different from that of the original text. What resulted were poems that couldn't really be called translations, nor could they be called original poems: they were half way between. Lowell called them "imitations."

Other poets have been more casual in turning foreign language poems into English. For example, look at the following poem by Giuseppe Ungaretti. (It doesn't matter if you don't understand Italian. Just look at the words.)

Tutto Ho Perduto

Tutto ho perduto dell'infanzia
E non potrò mai più
Smemorarmi in un grido.

L'infanzia ho sotterrato
Nel fondo delle notti
E ora, spada invisibile,
Mi separa da tutto.

Di me rammento che esultavo amandoti,
Ed eccomi perduto
In infinito delle notti.

Disperazione che incessante aumenta
La vita non mi è più,
Arrestata in fondo alla gola,
Che una roccia di gridi.

This is a serious poem about losing one's childhood and feeling lost in an infinity of nights. Poet Ted Berrigan, who knew almost no Italian, turned this poem into:

Tooting My Horn on Duty

Tooting my horn on duty in the infantry
Made my name mud   P-U!
In the army I had nosebleeds

The infantry was distracting
It kindled up in my nose
An invisible odor
That hindered my toots

One day while on duty I rammed into a chestnut
And got blood all over my flute
Not to mention this nosebleed

I spat out so many teeth I knew it was an omen
The vitamins I took made me ill
Ten blood transfusions! It was almost all over
When two big rocks stopped the bleeding

This then was my unhappy childhood

Notice that Berrigan focused on certain words and ignored others. He took *tutto* (which means "all" or "everything" in Italian) and translated it as *tooting*. He took *infanzia* ("infancy") and translated it as *infantry*, which probably made him see the word *army* in the last four letters of *smemorarmi*.

Berrigan's method is sometimes called intentional "mistranslation," that is, a translation error made on purpose. A more extreme type of mistranslation, in which the English version becomes more abstract and perhaps crazy, is when Pierre Reverdy's line "Un bonheur qui tremble encore est né" becomes "A bomb ear trembles in core of the knee."

If you understand even a little bit of a foreign language, try writing an imitation. You don't have to know any foreign language to do mistranslations. In either case, these kinds of poems are good to write because they teach you how to focus on the words, how they sound and fit together, and not to worry too much about the theme or subject. This is important, because ultimately poems are made not of feelings or ideas, but of words.

Insult Poem

"Your momma wears army boots!" "May you grow like an onion with your head in the ground." "Is that a head on your shoulders, or a button to keep your spine from unravelling?" These insults don't sound much like poetry, do they? And yet, they have a lot in common with a form of poetry called the "insult poem."

Like the chant, the insult poem has a repetitive form, but, unlike chants — which are usually concerned with primeval forces like love, hatred, and the weather — insult poems get personal. They're about somebody: your friend, your sister, your teacher, your classmate, your boss. Not only that, they're specific, telling that person some home truths about themselves that they might not have considered before. However, the biggest difference between a chant and an insult poem is that an insult poem is funny — it uses humor and exaggeration to get its point across, while a chant is serious, serious, serious.

The earliest recorded instances of the insult poem are from Africa, whose tribespeople have been making up and exchanging insult poems since time immemorial. For example:

> You really resemble
> An old man who has no teeth
> And who wants to eat elephant hide,
> Or a woman without a backside
> Who sits down on a hard wooden stool.
> You also resemble a stupid dolt
> Who while hunting lets an antelope pass by
> And who knows that his father is sick at home.

Not only is composing an insult poem a way to let out anger without fighting, it's a way to show off your verbal skill, and demonstrate your superiority with words, not fists. Some people think that the highly ritualized Black American form of "playing the dozens" — which involves people, usually young men, exchanging series of insults in a verbal battle, until one can't think of a come-back for the latest outrageous insult—has its roots in these African insults, which were probably familiar to some of the tribespeople brought to the U.S. as slaves in the eighteenth century.

To write an insult poem, you can't really be too angry at the person you're writing about — the idea is to have fun teasing them in a way that's affectionate but nasty enough to capture their attention. You might want to start with a harmless line, like "He's not so bad" or "Did you hear that...?", which will give you a launching pad for an ever more outrageous series of statements, as in the following example by a group of seventh-graders:

He's no so bad
He just killed his father by making him eat 10,000 fried chickens.
He's not so bad
He just plugged up his brother's tuba with his little sister.
He's not so bad
He just cleaned his little brother's nose with an electric
    toothbrush.
He's not so bad
He just fed his cat ballbearings and it sat on a magnet.

See also: CHANT, RAP.

Light Verse

Light verse is not a poetic form, it's a type of poetry. There are many varieties of it, including nonsense verse, limerick, parody, nursery rhymes, folk songs, occasional poems, alphabet poems, poems with lots of word play, epigrams, and what is called *vers de société* (French for "social verse"). *Vers de société* is brief, sophisticated, graceful, and witty poetry usually about social relationships and conventions. Like all light verse, *vers de société* expects its readers to understand it and find it agreeable to their way of looking at things. The poet W.H. Auden described light verse as "poetry which is simple, clear, and gay." In other words, it is not the poetry of an alienated, gloomy person who writes things that no one else can understand.

Light verse was popular in Greek and Latin classical literature. Many writers (including some who are thought of only as "serious" writers) have written light verse: among them, Aristophanes, Shakespeare, Goethe, Milton, Jonson, Pope, Lewis Carroll, T.S. Eliot, and Ogden Nash.

Because light verse can be written in so many different ways, it's impossible to give brief advice on how to write it and it's misleading to provide only an example or two. The best way to learn more about it is to read lots of it, beginning, perhaps, with *The Oxford Book of Light Verse*.

See also: ALPHABET POEM, EPIGRAM, LIMERICK, NONSENSE VERSE, OCCASIONAL POEM, PARODY.

Limerick

A man with a chest cold named Bill
Ingested a nuclear pill.
The doctor said "cough,"
The damn thing went off,
And they picked up Bill's head in Brazil.

That is a limerick, a five-line poem written in anapestic rhythm, with lines 1, 2, and 5 containing three beats and rhyming, and lines 3 and 4 containing two beats and rhyming.

No one is sure where the limerick originated. One theory is that soldiers returning from France brought it to the Irish town of Limerick in 1700. Another theory points to *Mother Goose Melodies for Children*, published in 1719, and to several limericks published shortly thereafter. Edward Lear (1812-1888) is renowned for establishing the limerick as an instrument of nonsense and comical verse, but many of his limericks fail to snap us with a sharp twist in the last line, a device that has characterized the best limericks since his time. The simplicity of Lear's limericks, however, endears them to us and makes them memorable.

There was an Old Lady whose folly
Induced her to sit on a holly,
Whereon, by a thorn,
Her dress being torn,
She quickly became melancholy.

*

There was a Young Lady of Poole,
Whose soup was excessively cool;
So she put it to boil
By the aid of some oil,
That ingenious Young Lady of Poole.

An acceptable limerick can follow Lear's tradition of starting each verse with "There was...," but exceptional limericks will probably explore a more immediate way to start the poem. The first of Lear's limericks cited above is probably the better of the two because the last line explores a new rhyme and advances the narrative, rather than settling on repetition that renders the poem only four lines of information.

Limericks are frequently bawdy jokes, off-color poems whose delight is in rhythm and rhyme being employed for naughty purposes.

> A limerick packs laughs anatomical
> Into space that is quite economical.
> But the good ones I've seen
> So seldom are clean,
> And the clean ones so seldom are comical.

Implicit in the limerick's rhyme-and-rhythm-associated-with-humor is a challenge: can anyone write a limerick that does not seem to be trying for a laugh? Is a "serious limerick" possible? How can one take that familiar da da ta, da da ta, da ta rhythm and mute it sufficiently that the words of a poem create a somber response? How about a serious limerick on the subject of death?

See also: RHYTHM, LIGHT VERSE.

Line

When most of us think of a poem, we imagine it on a page looking very different from prose. In some poems, there will be differences in capitalization and punctuation. But the most obvious difference is in the line. Most poems don't extend all the way from margin to margin, and some differ in length from line to line. For instance, we recognize that the following is poetry because of the way it is arranged on the page:

All the leaves
are down except
the ones that aren't.
They shake or
a wind shakes
them but they
won't go oh
no there goes
one now. No.
It's a bird
batting by.
         —*From "Verge" by James Schuyler*

We also know it's poetry because of the way the lines are arranged to emphasize and complement the musical elements of the language.

How does the poet determine the length of each line? There is either some "measure" (see RHYTHM and FOOT) or else we say that the poem is *free verse*. Let's consider the poem in measure first. If someone reads the following to you and asks you to arrange it in lines, you would probably have no difficulty doing so.

Hickory, dickory, dock.
The mouse ran up the clock.
The clock struck one
And down he run;
Hickory, dickory, dock.

You can hear how long these lines are, and you could probably even fill in the measure with words of your own. This nursery rhyme demonstrates several of the many patterns that are common in our language. Perhaps the most common line in English is iambic pentameter (a line of ten syllables, with five accents, an unaccented syllable followed by an accented one). See if you can hear the rhythmic pattern — just as you could hear "Hickory dickory dock" — in the following lines from William Wordsworth's "Michael":

> Upon the Forest-side in Grasmere Vale
> There dwelt a Shepherd, Michael was his name,
> An old man, stout of heart, and strong of limb.
> His bodily frame had been from youth to age
> Of an unusual strength; his mind was keen
> Intense and frugal, apt for all affairs,
> And in his Shepherd's calling he was prompt
> And watchful more than ordinary men.

At first this is a little harder to imitate, because the line now attempts to sound like speech instead of sing-song, with the subtler and more abundant variations of measure and accent that we hear when we listen to someone talk. To promote greater variety within lines of equal length and measure, Wordsworth uses commas and a semicolon to insert pauses within the lines (as well as at the end of two of them). Such pauses within lines are called *caesuras,* and are usually indicated by punctuation. There can be more than one caesura within a line, as in

> An old man, stout of heart, and strong of limb.

To quicken the pace of a poem, you can break the line so that it pulls the reader into the next line. In the excerpt from "Verge," you see examples of such *enjambment* in four consecutive lines:

> a wind shakes
> them but they
> won't go oh
> no there goes
> one now. No.

From line to line the reader rushes from *shakes* to *them,* *they* to *won't,* *oh* to *no,* and *goes* to *one,* the poem continuing to pick up speed. Then the caesura in the last line interrupts this breathless rush.

The poet Charles Olson followed Wordsworth's lead, insisting that the line be determined by the breath of the particular poet. Because the pulse, rate of breathing, and regional accent varies from person to person, Olson thought you should be able to perceive the biological signature of the poet in his or her lines. But not all poets write poems to imitate talking. Walt Whitman, perhaps the greatest American poet, adapted the colorful language of the stump orator and the crusading editor with the exalted Biblical rhythms of the King James version of the Psalms to produce a new kind of democratic chant, an idiomatic and quirky but familiar rhythmic measure:

> When the psalm sings instead of the singer,
> When the script preaches instead of the preacher,
> When the pulpit descends and goes instead of the carver that
>   carved the supporting desk,
> When the sacred vessels or the bits of the eucharist, or the lath
>   and plast, procreate as effectually as the young silversmiths
>   or bakers, or the masons in their overalls,
> When a university course convinces like a slumbering woman and
>   child convince,
> When the minted gold in the vault smiles like the nightwatchman's
>   daughter,
> When warrantee deeds loafe in chairs opposite and are my
>   friendly companions,
> I intend to reach them my hand and make as much of them as I
>   do of men and women.
>   —*From* Leaves of Grass

Because this line is so sustained and long-limbed, some people can't hear the measure in it. (In fact, many of these lines are so long that they run over the margins of the printed page. When that happens, the poetic line is continued on the next printed line, but is indented, as here, or in some other way marked to show that it is a continuation and not a new line.) A line this long demands a patient attention, and for some readers breaks down into shorter units. Some ears might prefer the fourth line above divided into more compact lines:

When the sacred vessels
or the bits of the eucharist,
or the lath and plast,
procreate as effectually
as the young silversmiths or bakers,
or the masons in their overalls

Can you see how this change in the line arrangement affects the speed and emphasis with which you read the passage?

The number of ways to determine the length of a poetic line are almost as many as the number of poets. Marianne Moore wrote poems in which the lines were determined according to the number of syllables in each, with the same pattern applying to separate stanzas. Jack Collom's lunes specify the number of words in each line. And of course there is also free verse where you can do anything you want.

Some poets don't even bother with the line, writing prose poems or free prose. Others continue to rely on traditional forms, in which the line conforms to some traditional accentual or numerical measure. With the increasing dissemination of poetry via cassette, radio, and record, some poets treat line breaks primarily as reading instructions for oral performance.

Finally, many poets consider the arrangement of the poem on the page the equivalent of musical notation — the best means to indicate how the reader might hear the poem just like the poet did, before it was written anywhere except on the wind.

See also: FREE VERSE, FOOT, LINE, PROJECTIVE VERSE, RHYTHM,
       SYLLABIC VERSE.

List poem

The list poem (also called "catalog poem") is a very old form of poetry. It consists of an itemization of things or events. List poems can be of any length, rhymed or unrhymed. The original purpose of this descriptive, repetitive verse was often functional. For instance, Polynesian list poems formed an inventory of all the islands in Polynesia. List poems have also been used as a hybrid of history and entertainment, as in Book II of Homer's *Iliad,* in which the poet lists all the major Greek heroes come to fight in the Trojan War. In the Bible, the book of Genesis can be seen as a list poem that traces the lineage of Adam's family.

Another popular type of list poem, the *blazon*, itemizes the qualities of a loved one, whose teeth are compared to pearls, lips to ripe cherries, etc. Unless such praise is presented skillfully, it can grow boring. The French Surrealist poet André Breton took the blazon to interesting extremes in his "Free Union" (1931), which begins:

> My woman with her forest-fire hair
> With her heat-lightning thoughts
> With her hourglass waist
> My woman with her otter waist in the tiger's mouth
> My woman with her rosette mouth a bouquet of stars of the
>   greatest magnitude
> With her teeth of white mouse footprints on the white earth
> With her tongue of polished amber and glass
> My woman with her stabbed eucharist tongue
> With her tongue of a doll that opens and closes its eyes
> With her tongue of incredible stone
> My woman with her eyelashes in a child's handwriting
> With her eyebrows the edge of a swallow's nest
> My woman with her temples of a greenhouse with a slate roof
> And steam on the windowpanes
> My woman with her shoulders of champagne
> And a dolphin-headed fountain under ice
> My woman with her matchstick wrists
> My woman with her lucky fingers her ace of hearts fingers
> With her fingers of new-mown hay
>   — *Translated by Bill Zavatsky and Zack Rogow*

Another type of list poem presents a series of events or activities. Christopher Smart, in his poem "Jubilate Agno" (about his cat Geoffrey), describes how Geoffrey gets up in the morning and goes through a little religious ritual. Then, having considered God, Geoffrey considers himself:

> For first he looks upon his fore-paws to see if they are clean.
> For secondly he kicks up behind to clear away there.
> For thirdly he works it upon stretch with the fore-paws extended.
> For fourthly he sharpens his paws by wood.
> For fifthly he washes himself.
> For sixthly he rolls upon wash.
> For seventhly he fleas himself, that he may not be
>   interrupted upon the beat.
> For eighthly he rubs himself against a post.
> For ninthly he looks up for his instructions.
> For tenthly he goes in quest of food.

In what is probably the best-known modern epic poem, *Leaves of Grass*, Walt Whitman uses lists expansively. Whitman appears at first to include examples of people from all walks of life. But as Kenneth Koch pointed out in *Sleeping on the Wing*, Whitman deliberately left out negative images, especially satanic or evil ones. This helps us understand how Whitman's inventory was given dimension through his positive, celebratory tone.

In our own time, Allen Ginsberg has created a similar epic poem, "Howl." Although the images he chooses to record are energetic (like Whitman's), they are not all positive. In fact, nearly every image is undercut by some disturbing aspect, some sense of decay and waste.

The famous opening lines of "Howl" set the stage for the rest of the poem, which is largely a description of Ginsberg's friends and experience:

> I have seen the best minds of my generation[. . .]
> who bared their brains to heaven[. . .]
> who passed through universities with radiant cool eyes[. . .]
> who were expelled from the academies[. . .]
> who ate fire[. . .]

who sank all night in submarine light[. . .]
who talked continuously[. . .]
who wandered around and around at midnight[. . .]
[etc.]

"Howl" is a good model for students. It invites an author to draw details from his or her own life and offers a simple organizational structure. Also, its speed and inventive phrasing pose a challenge to an author to keep the work lively and moving.

Ted Berrigan includes everyday items in his often funny list poems, such as "10 Things I Do Every Day," "Things to Do at Anne's," and "Things to Do in Providence."

The list poem is one of the most popular and enduring forms. It is particularly suitable for people just beginning to write poetry, because its form is flexible and its content has authenticity by virtue of its often being derived from the writer's personal experience.

Lune
("LOON")

The lune is a short form invented and named by poet Robert Kelly in the 1960s out of a dissatisfaction with our Western use of haiku. Since English says things in fewer syllables than does Japanese, he reasoned that a shorter English pattern would be appropriate to the haiku-size thought. He experimented and settled on a thirteen-syllable form arranged 5 / 3 / 5 in three lines. He called it "lune" (French for "moon") because the righthand, varying edge of it is bowed like a crescent moon, and also because it reminded him of the number of lunar months in a year (thirteen).

Here are two poems by Robert Kelly from a series called "Knee Lunes." The first refers to the knees.

they are given to
hold close, not
air, not each other

*

thin sliver of the
crescent moon
high up the real world

Kelly emphasizes the form's simplicity by omitting capitalization and end punctuation, but that's not part of the form.

A variant form of the lune arose through a mistake. Poet Jack Collom, beginning to work with schoolchildren, misremembered Kelly's idea as a count of 3 / 5 / 3 *words*, not syllables. He liked it that way, feeling that it would be more flexible than haiku and that children would, counting words, not get as caught up in the mere mechanics. So thousands of children and others have worked with that pattern. Here are a few examples of kids' lunes:

A raindrop falls.
It falls on my nose —
delicate, light, transparent.

*

Think of me
as a beautiful ballerina twirling
around the block.

*

Rock shock the
house. Everybody to the funky
beat, yes yes.

*

Remember me, remember
me. Put it all together
and remember me.

The lune poem is not limited by haiku traditions, such as referring to a season. Lunes can be very American, colloquial, almost anything imagination brings that can be squeezed into eleven words so divided into lines. The shortness forces a fine attention on the tiny effects in language, as in the raindrop piece where the clownish second line suddenly flowers into precise romance and subtle rhythm in the third. In such brevity, any awkward rhythm or syntax sticks out like a very sore thumb. Thus lunes remind us that ideas depend on aesthetic subtleties for their very being.

It is important to read a large variety of good lunes aloud, noticing the details as you go, so that you are brought into a closeup on each word and also into a 3 / 5 / 3 mental rhythm. One junior high school girl wrote 120 lunes in one night. During a period of protracted involvement, the mind can develop temporary mental molds for thought so that every idea or sight comes 3 / 5 / 3 in words.

Lunes may be quite experimental or, on the other hand, quite simple. The variety possible in these eleven-word (or thirteen-syllable) poems is astonishing.

See also: HAIKU.

Lyric
("LEAR-ic")

The word *lyric* comes from the ancient Greek musical instrument, the lyre. When Greek poets sang or recited poems, they often accompanied themselves on the lyre — a small, portable stringed instrument like a small harp. In the Renaissance, many poems were sung to the accompaniment of the lute; today the closest thing we have to the lute is the guitar.

Here is an example of a lyric poem from John Dowland's *First Booke of Songs* (1597), which was also the first English publication for solo voice and lute (and other stringed instruments):

Dear, If You Change

Dear, if you change, I'll never choose again.
Sweet, if you shrink, I'll never think of love.
Fair, if you fail, I'll judge all beauty vain.
Wise, if too weak, more wits I'll never prove.
Dear, Sweet, Fair, Wise, change, shrink, nor be not weak:
And, on my faith, my faith shall never break.

Earth with her flow'rs shall sooner heav'n adorn,
Heav'n her bright stars through earth's dim globe shall move,
Fire heat shall lose, and frost of flames be born,
Air made to shine as black as hell shall prove:
Earth, Heaven, Fire, Air, the world transform'd shall view,
Ere I prove false to faith, or strange to you.

For the last 500 years or so, poets have increasingly written lyric poems that are not intended for musical accompaniment. But lyric poems continue to resemble songs in three important ways: 1) they are shorter than dramatic or epic poems; 2) they tend to express the personal feelings of one speaker, often the poet; and 3) they give you the feeling that they *could* be sung.

Lyric poems always express some emotion, and no matter how artful the lyric poet, he or she can't disguise that he or she is a mere mortal, with passions, follies, enthusiasms. Lyric poems are intimate in a way that conventional public expressions are not, which may be why many lyric poets are shy about reading their poems except to their closest friends.

Usually the lyric poet is speaking in his or her own voice, but there are also dramatic lyrics, where the poet writes a monologue in the voice of another character. A good example of a dramatic lyric is "My Last Duchess" by Robert Browning. Since the beginning of the nineteenth century, artists have been breaking down the barriers between different artistic genres, and so, in addition to dramatic lyrics, you will discover lyric epics, epic dramas, etc. Subjects like philosophy and poetry itself, which some poets don't consider proper for lyric poems, have always been incorporated in poems by poets who felt as passionately about ideas or art as about love or death. You will also come across critics who have formulated theories of the lyric that try to confine it to what it has been in the past. However, the things that poets feel strongly enough to sing about will change from poet to poet, from generation to generation, from town to town.

Here is an example of a lyric poem by Zachery Linton (age twelve).

Paradise in Disguise

Harlem is like Paradise
in disguise
but you have to look
not with your eyes.
Flow, love of life, but
neighbor is what it's built on

These things do happen
but it is short-lived
because fire from a pipe
won't keep you happy
    Living in Paradise
is living in Harlem
despite evil things it's still
nice

You have to look with
eagle eyes at things
    that are in disguise
the crazy, evil, threatening
things.

See also: ODE.

Macaronic Verse
("mack-uh-RON-ic")

Macaronic verse is a peculiar, rare, and often comic form of poetry that sometimes borders on nonsense. It is the mixture of two (or more) languages in a poem, in which the poet usually subjects one language to the grammatical laws of another to make people laugh. The word *macaronic* comes from the Italian word *maccaroni*, which, yes, means macaroni.

In the past, macaronic verse was usually written by mixing Latin with one other language. It is thought that the form was invented by a poet named Tisi degli Odassi who mixed Latin with Italian in his *Carmen maccaronicum* (Macaronic Songs) in 1488.

During the fifteenth century, and for a time before and after that, many poets wrote both in Latin and in the language they spoke every day. Latin is in some ways a high-toned language, and at that time it was used by educated people only. A revolution began to take place in which poets wrote mainly in the everyday language all the people used, which is called the "vernacular" language of their country. While this revolution was taking place, macaronic verse provided a way to make fun of a number of things: the Latin language, education, and pretentious people.

One of the funniest examples of macaronic verse is the finale of "The Imaginary Invalid," a play by the seventeenth-century poet Molière. The play is about a hypochondriac and ends with a comic ceremony involving eight men bearing syringes, six druggists, twenty-two doctors, one medical student, eight surgeons dancing and two surgeons singing.

SECOND SURGEON:
    May all his anni
    Be to him boni
    And favorable ever
    Et n'habere never
    Quam plaguas, poxas,
    Fievras, pluresias
    Bloody effusions and dissenterias.

113

CHORUS:

> Vivat, vivat, vivat, vivat, for ever vivat
> Novus doctor, qui tam bene speakat,
> Mille, mille annis, and manget and bibat,
> Et bleedat and killat.

It's hard to "translate" this funny verse because there are no such words as *bleedat* and *killat*. Loosely, it means: "May all his years be good to him and ever favorable, and may he never not have plagues, poxes, fevers, pleurisies, bloody effusions, and dysenteries. Let him live, live, live, live, let him live forever, new doctor, for thousands and thousands of years, and let him eat and drink and be bled and killed."

This kind of writing is a form of satire. It is also a way to practice and discover how poetry can make new words, in this case wild and silly and nonsensical ones out of more than one language. Here are two more examples:

> Me wretched! Let me curr to quercine shades!
> Effund your albid hausts, lactiferous maids!
> Oh, might I vole to some umbrageous chump, —
> Depart, —be off, —excede, —evade, —erump!
> — *Oliver Wendell Holmes, from "Aestivation"*

> Qui nunc dancere vult modo
> Wants to dance in the fashion, oh!
> Discere debet — ought to know,
> Kickere floor cum heel et toe
>   One, two, three,
>   Hop with me,
> Whirligig, twirligig, rapidé.
> — *Gilbert Abbott à Becket, from "A Holiday Task"*

The idea of macaronic verse can be expanded on in many ways today: if you know more than one language, you can mix languages together in ways that are beautiful, as in eight-year-old Ilona Baburka's poem:

The León in Invierno

One invierno a león came to the nieve bosque.
And walked in the bosque and his garra was in the deep la
   paloma white nieve.
The trees had like white nieve platos on the branch.
And it was Navidad la noche and the violeto cielo was full of
   baile estrellas.

Translation: **The Lion in Winter**

One winter a lion came to the snowy woods.
And walked in the woods, and his paw was in the deep dovey
   white snow.
The trees had like white snowy dishes on the branch.
And it was Christmas Night and the violet sky was full of
   dancing stars.

You can also write variations of the macaronic by writing a poem
that mixes different kinds of one language, such as the language of a
textbook mixed with the language of people talking, or what your
friends say mixed with what your parents say, or phrases from the
newspaper intermingled with your own thoughts about love.

See also: CENTO.

Madrigal
("MAD-rih-gahl")

Madrigals are poems written to be set to music. Although madrigals are usually love poems, they can be about anything. Usually they are short, the language, ideas, and images fairly simple. (The word *madrigal* comes from a Latin word meaning "something simple.") This simplicity makes it easier for the composer to make the musical ideas correspond to or contrast with the literary ideas.

The madrigal is an old form. In the fourteenth century, when madrigals originated, they followed a strict form. The early madrigals of northern Italy were composed of two or three tercets (three-line verses) followed by one or two rhyming couplets (two-line verses). All the lines were of seven or eight syllables. But later the madrigal became a much freer form and the only thing that remained consistent was the final rhyming couplet. In modern times even that has been abandoned.

The example below is by the English poet John Farmer, written in 1599 when madrigals were extremely popular in England.

> Fair Phyllis I saw sitting all alone
>   Feeding her flock near the mountain side.
> The shepherds knew not whither she was gone
>   But after her Amyntas hied.
> Up and down he wandered whilst she was missing;
> When he found her, O, then they fell a-kissing.

Farmer's musical setting of "Fair Phyllis" is for four voices. The soprano voice takes the lead, with the other three voices joining in at the second line. Eventually Farmer plays the voices off each other, some voices singing together in harmony, others singing against them, the words either slightly behind or slightly ahead, repeating lines and varying them. Sung twice through, the final version has the four voices all finishing "a-kissing" at the same time. The whole effect is very rich and complex.

When writing a madrigal, you have to keep to a fairly consistent rhythm and perhaps rhyme scheme (including the final couplet). Madrigals are meant to be *sung*, so the words shouldn't be too long or difficult for a singer to pronounce or make understood to an audience. You might want to test your madrigal with some singers. You might even want to collaborate with the composer while you are still writing the words, to see how the composer responds to your words musically and to discover whether or not what he or she comes up with inspires you to change what you've already written.

See also: LYRIC.

Metaphor
(''MET-uh-for'')

The word *metaphor* is a combination of two ancient Greek words: *meta* ("beyond, across, over") and *phoreo* ("to carry, bring, bear"). If you lived in Greece today, you would see this word—METAPHORA —on the sides of moving vans, a good way to remember what it means. A *metaphor* is a figure of speech in which the qualities of one thing are carried over to another thing, the way the furniture from one house is moved by truck to another house.

And so the metaphor always contains two parts, an X and a Y. The poet wants to create an equals sign between them: X = Y. Many poets find "similarities" between things that are often quite different: waves crashing on the beach look like knives; wave = knife. Poets also create metaphors to express feelings. They compare what they feel to something that resembles it. A feeling of sadness, for example, may lead us to think of a gray, rainy day: sadness = rain. We could express these pictures in our mind by writing, "The rain is my sadness," or, "Sadness falls inside me like the rain." By taking our feelings, which are sometimes unclear to us, and finding an object or an action that expresses them, we sharpen our own understanding of ourselves and can pass that understanding on to people who have similar feelings.

The metaphor, then, is a powerful means of expressing ideas and feelings that might otherwise remain unspoken, unwritten, or undiscovered.

Metaphor and Image
In modern times the metaphor has often been called the "image." Around 1910 a small group of poets in London, centered around the poet Ezra Pound and the philosopher T.E. Hulme, decided that

poetry should have strong images (metaphors), and that these metaphors must be the heart of their poems. Here is perhaps the most famous Imagist poem, by Ezra Pound:

In a Station of the Metro

The apparition of these faces in the crowd;
Petals on a wet, black bough.

But let's stop for a moment and talk a little about the word "imagination." Imagination means, first and foremost, the ability to create mental images — pictures in our minds. But where do these mind-pictures come from? First of all, they come from our experience: the things that we have seen, touched, smelled, heard, tasted, and thought about. They come from *memory*. Each of us has thousands of memory-pictures stored up in our minds. Writers learn how to remember, and how to turn these memory-pictures (and sounds and smells) into words.

Another source of word-pictures comes from the practice of *observation*. If you were to look out your window and write about everything that passed by, even if it was the cars moving down the street or leaves blowing across the yard, you would be putting images on paper. Writers work to become sharp-eyed observers as well as great rememberers.

A photograph or a drawing of a rose is an *image* of a rose, and not the real rose. In using language, we have taken away the picture and replaced it with a word that stands for it. The four letters that make up the word "rose" don't look like the flower, and yet the word calls up a picture of that flower in our minds. What we are talking about, then, are the pictures in the mind (called mental images) that words have the power to make us "see." We "see" these images, as Shakespeare said, with the "mind's eye." The pictures that we see when we remember something that happened to us — the beach we visited last summer — and the things that we see in dreams are also "mental images."

Word-pictures that come from memories or from the observation of things that are happening right in front of us are *realistic*. Another meaning of the word "imagination" involves making up things that have never existed. Walt Disney's cartoon movie *Fantasia* shows us

119

elephants dancing on soap bubbles. We know that no such thing can really happen, but, presto, there it is on the screen! This is a *fantasy* image. Because it combines two different things, the metaphor is a creation of fantasy: metaphors exist only in poems, works of art, and in our minds, but they are very powerful because they bring into existence things that can't be put on a table in front of us.

Therefore, the rose that we have been talking about is only the X or Y in our equation; to create a metaphor, another second element is needed.

The metaphor, as we have seen, is a combination of *two* ideas — wave and knife, or sadness and rain. If a rose reminds us of a pretty face (face = rose), by joining them we then create a *third* thing — the metaphor.

While the face that is also a rose isn't real in the same way that a single rose or a particular girl's face is real, it nevertheless can exist in our minds as an idea or a picture. We could take a color photograph of a rose and the photograph of a girl's face, and print the face on the rose. Or we could draw a rose, and shape it into a girl's face. So it is possible to see two images in our mind, combine them, and put the combination into words. The result is a metaphor.

Kinds of Metaphor

The word *metaphor* has a general meaning, as shown in the four categories below. It also has a specific meaning, as discussed in the second category below.

• X *is like* Y. "My love is like a red, red rose."
This kind of metaphor is called a *simile* (from the Latin word *similis*, meaning "like" or "similar"). The simile always uses the words "like" or "as" to connect two things.

• X *is* Y. "My love is a red rose."
This figure of speech is called a *metaphor* to separate it from the *simile*. It creates the same effect by bringing two things together, without using "like" or "as."

• X *of* Y. "Girl of rose."
The idea here is that X *is made out of* Y. This kind of metaphor is quite common. Superman is known as the "Man of Steel." A mean

person is often said to have a "heart of stone." A popular song of a few years back was called "Heart of Glass," meaning that whoever had one had sensitive feelings that were easily shattered.

- XY. "Girl-rose" or "rose-girl."

Here the two words are joined together, usually with a hyphen. In one early English poem the sea is called the "whale-road," because this is the path taken by the whale. This type of metaphor has a special name, taken from the one that the Old English poets gave it; it is called a *kenning*. The word "ken" is still in our dictionaries, and is used in expressions like "out of my ken," meaning "out of my sight or knowledge." If something is "out of your ken," you don't see it or understand it. To "ken" something means to "know" something. A "kenning" is a "knowing," and the metaphor is a knowing—of how two different things are in some ways the same. In the metaphor, a *recognition* takes place: the sea is the road of the whales; this girl is a rose.

Nonsense Verse

Nonsense verse is poetry that doesn't make sense, but it isn't just formless gibberish. For example,

eyu.;w/ k.l ..yvv;uo:–
rt"dxk,'qqq
d
l.shr,)
fpb

is not an example of nonsense verse, whereas the following is:

A Tetrastich in the Lanternish Language

Briszmarg dalgotbrick nubstzne zos,
Isquebsz prusq: albok crinqs zacbac.
Mizbe dilbarskz morp nipp stancz bos,
Strombtz, Panurge, walmap quost gruszbac.
— *François Rabelais*

Rabelais' lines are of a regular length, the punctuation is consistent, and the lines rhyme. It gives us the feeling that if we only understood Lanternish we would understand the poem. That's the trick: Lanternish is a language complete with its own rules, but we will never be able to understand it because it is a made-up language. True nonsense verse gives us the feeling that it comes from a world different from ours, a world with its own rules, as in this anonymous nonsense poem:

There was a man of Thessaly,
　And he was wondrous wise,
He jumped into a bramble bush
　And scratched out both his eyes.
And when he saw his eyes were out,
　With all his might and main
He jumped into another bush
　And scratched them in again.

122

Although this poem is in clear English, its logic is alien. Like the Lanternish above, however, it is perfectly consistent. We know it doesn't make sense, but we delight in it.

All good nonsense verse tickles the mind and gives delight. The most quoted nonsense verses are probably certain nursery rhymes and anonymous folk poetry, such as

> What's your name?
> Puddin Tane.
> Ask me again
> And I'll tell you the same.

Perhaps the most famous printed nonsense poem is Lewis Carroll's "The Jabberwocky." Other good writers of nonsense verse are Edward Lear, Walter de la Mare, Christian Morgenstern, and Stevie Smith.

Good nonsense verse is surprisingly hard to write. It requires that the author keep the poem consistent while at the same time letting it be crazy. It's not hard to be consistent and it's not hard to write crazily, but it's hard to do both at the same time, and have the result be light, tantalizing, and satisfying. Also, there's a fine line between good nonsense and plain silliness.

As with most poetic forms, one of the best ways to learn to write it is to read lots of it. You'll be more attracted to some types of nonsense verse than to others; they'll seem more natural to you. These are the first ones to try writing yourself. Then, as you write, don't worry about the result. Instead, let yourself get all the way into the world of the poem. To test your poem, read it to children and see what they think of it.

See also: LIGHT VERSE.

Occasional Poem

Occasional poetry is poetry written for a specific occasion about a particular event, including weddings, funerals, and birthdays. Occasional poems can also celebrate or memorialize military, athletic, and political events. Occasional poems can be long or short, in strict forms or in free verse.

The ancient Greek poet Pindar wrote odes to celebrate the victors of athletic competitions. Many English poets have written epithalamiums to celebrate weddings. John Milton's *Lycidas* was an elegy for a young man. Storytellers, poets, and minstrels have always had their say about what was going on; when printing became accessible, writers began distributing topical poems and ballads on one-page sheets, called "broadsides."

Topical poets and songwriters such as Woody Guthrie, Phil Ochs, Allen Ginsberg, Robert Bly, and Bob Dylan have written on subjects ranging from plane crashes to the Vietnamese War to racial segregation. When such occasional works complain about an existing social situation and suggest a change, they are also called *protest* songs or poems.

The only rule for writing an occasional poem is that you must pick an occasion to write about or for. There is one advantage in having a group write an occasional poem together: since the occasion belongs to everyone by being public, the poem can gain strength from being the expression of everyone's feelings. For example, groups of students have written birthday poems for their teachers, dedication poems for rooms added to the school and for playground renovations, and elegies for people whose deaths affected everyone.

See also: EPITHALAMIUM, ELEGY, ODE, COLLABORATION.

Ode
("OWED")

The ode form has undergone so many modifications that it nearly defies definition. An early writer on the ode, Edmund Gosse, defined the ode as any type of "enthusiastic and exalted lyrical verse, directed to a fixed purpose and dealing progressively with one dignified theme." The word *ode* comes from the Greek word *aeidein* ("to sing"), and an ode is a song, a lyric poem, most often one that addresses a thing or person not present.

The Greek poet Pindar (522-442 B.C.) is credited with inventing the ode. He was commissioned to write them for particular occasions; they were sung and danced by a chorus. Each of Pindar's victory odes (which commemorate the victor of an athletic competition and are the only odes of Pindar to survive intact) includes a formal beginning, an invocation, prayer, myth, a moral and a conclusion, all in complicated metrical and stanzaic patterns, although according to his translator Richmond Lattimore, Pindar strove for spontaneity just the same. The tone is exalted and intense.

Another type of ode was written by the Roman poet Horace (65-8 B.C.). His odes were calmer, more philosophical, more personal, sometimes briefer. Like Pindar's, they followed particular stanzaic and metrical patterns.

Scholars generally agree that there are three types of English odes: Pindaric, Horatian, and Irregular. The Horatian ode, unlike the Pindaric, contains one stanza pattern that is repeated throughout the poem. An example of this is Alexander Pope's "Ode on Solitude":

Ode on Solitude

Happy the man whose wish and care
A few paternal acres bound,
Content to breathe his native air
           In his own ground.

Whose herds with milk, whose fields with bread,
Whose flocks supply him with attire;
Whose trees in summer yield him shade,
   In winter fire.

Blessed, who can unconcern'dly find
Hours, days, and years slide soft away
In health of body, peace of mind,
   Quiet by day,

Sound sleep by night; study and ease
Together mixed; sweet recreation,
And innocence, which most does please
   With meditation.

Thus let me live, unseen, unknown;
Thus unlamented let me die;
Steal from the world, and not a stone
   Tell where I lie.

His is not a poem that needs to be performed, but may be enjoyed more quietly in private, with time for reflection.

The third form of the ode, the Irregular ode, opens wide the doors of formal possibilities, for some or all of the metrical, stanzaic, and line regulations may be discarded, to the point that all that remains of the ode is its rise and fall of emotional intensity and its dedication to one dignified subject. Although the odes of Keats and Shelley, and Wordsworth's "Ode: Intimations of Immortality from Recollections of Early Childhood" are examples of this kind of ode, they have the tone and certain thematic elements of classical tradition, as well as their own rules of form. Here is one of Keats' odes:

Ode on a Grecian Urn

Thou still unravished bride of quietness,
 Thou foster child of silence and slow time,
Sylvan historian, who canst thus express
 A flowery tale more sweetly than our rhyme:
What leaf-fringed legend haunts about thy shape
 Of deities or mortals, or of both,
  In Tempe or the dales of Arcady?

What men or gods are these? What maidens loath?
  What mad pursuit? What struggle to escape?
    What pipes and timbrels? What wild ecstasy?

Heard melodies are sweet, but those unheard
  Are sweeter; therefore, ye soft pipes, play on;
Not to the sensual ear, but, more endeared,
  Pipe to the spirit ditties of no tone.
Fair youth, beneath the trees, thou canst not leave
  Thy song, nor ever can those trees be bare;
    Bold Lover, never, never canst thou kiss,
Though winning near the goal — yet, do not grieve;
  She cannot fade, though thou hast not thy bliss
    Forever wilt thou love, and she be fair!

Ah, happy, happy boughs! that cannot shed
  Your leaves, nor ever bid the Spring adieu;
And, happy melodist, unwearied,
  Forever piping songs forever new;
More happy love! more happy, happy love!
  Forever warm and still to be enjoyed,
    Forever panting, and forever young;
All breathing human passion far above,
  That leaves a heart high-sorrowful and cloyed,
    A burning forehead, and a parching tongue.

Who are these coming to the sacrifice?
  To what green altar, O mysterious priest,
Lead'st thou that heifer lowing at the skies,
  And all her silken flanks with garlands dressed?
What little town by river or sea shore,
  Or mountain-built with peaceful citadel,
    Is emptied of this folk, this pious morn?
And, little town, thy streets for evermore
  Will silent be; and not a soul to tell
    Why thou art desolate, can e'er return.

O Attic shape! Fair attitude! with brede
  Of marble men and maidens overwrought,
With forest branches and the trodden weed;
  Thou, silent form, dost tease us out of thought
As doth eternity. Cold Pastoral!
  When old age shall this generation waste,
    Thou shalt remain, in midst of other woe

Than ours, a friend to man, to whom thou say'st,
   "Beauty is truth, truth beauty" — that is all
      Ye know on earth, and all ye need to know.

The Chilean poet Pablo Neruda (1904-1973) takes the Irregular Ode a step further by disregarding the calling for a dignified theme. Neruda brings the lofty ode down to earth, so to speak, in his *Odas Elementales (Odes to Simple Things)*. Younger writers in particular enjoy writing this kind of ode, in which they use exalted language to write about a down-to-earth object, because the object keeps the poem's atmosphere from getting the stuffiness that exalted language sometimes brings. Here is Neruda's "Ode to the Watermelon":

Ode to the Watermelon

The tree of intense
summer,
hard,
is all blue sky,
yellow sun,
fatigue in drops,
a sword
above the highways,
a scorched shoe
in the cities:
the brightness and the world
weigh us down,
hit us
in the eyes
with clouds of dust,
with sudden golden blows,
they torture
our feet
with tiny thorns,
with hot stones,
and the mouth
suffers
more than all the toes:
the throat
becomes thirsty,

the teeth,
the lips, the tongue:
we want to drink
waterfalls,
the dark blue night,
the South Pole,
and then
the coolest of all
the planets crosses
the sky,
the round, magnificent,
star-filled watermelon.

It's a fruit from the thirst-tree.
It's the green whale of the summer.
The dry universe
all at once
given dark stars
by this firmament of coolness
lets the swelling
fruit
come down:
its hemispheres open
showing a flag
green, white, red,
that dissolves into
wild rivers, sugar,
delight!

Jewel box of water, phlegmatic
queen
of the fruitshops,
warehouse
of profundity, moon
on earth!
You are pure,
rubies fall apart
in your abundance,
and we
want
to bite into you,
to bury our
face
in you, and

the soul!
When we're thirsty
we glimpse you
like
a mine or a mountain
of fantastic food,
but
among our longings and our teeth
you change
simply
into cool light
that slips in turn into
spring water
that touched us once
singing.
And that is why
you don't weigh us down
in the siesta hour
that's like an oven,
you don't weigh us down,
you just
go by
and your heart, some cold ember,
turned itself into a single
drop of water.
         — *Translated by Robert Bly*

Other notable modern odes are Allen Tate's "Ode to the Confederate Dead," W.H. Auden's "In Memory of W.B. Yeats," and those of Frank O'Hara. Ultimately what has survived of the ode in its 2,500 years is its spontaneity, its expansiveness, and its openness to a wide range of emotions. Perhaps rather than its formal attributes, these are the qualities that make an ode an ode.

See also: LYRIC.

Ottava Rima
("o-TAH-vah REE-ma")

Ottava rima (from Italian, meaning roughly "rhyme in eights") is a stanza of eight lines that rhyme *abababcc*. In English the lines follow the rhythmical pattern of iambic pentameter. Here's a contemporary example of a stanza in ottava rima:

> One night in Venice, near the Grand Canal,
> A lovely girl was sitting by her stoop.
> Sixteen years old, Elizabeth Gedall,
> When, suddenly, a giant ice-cream scoop
> Descended from the clouded blue corral
> Of heaven and scooped her skyward with a loop-
> The-loopy motion, which the gods of Venice
> Saw, and, enraged, they left off cosmic tennis....
> — *From* The Duplications *by Kenneth Koch*

Ottava rima had been used in thirteenth-century Italian religious verse, but in the next century the Italian poet Giovanni Boccaccio adapted it for more purely artistic purposes to tell long and interesting stories. In the early sixteenth century, Ludovico Ariosto used ottava rima in his epic poem *Orlando Furioso (Frenzied Roland)*, a wonderfully long and rich work that mixes the comic and the serious, story and commentary, history and fantasies that include flying horses, knights and maidens, and a trip to the moon.

Other poets of the Renaissance—Italian, Spanish, Portuguese, and English — also used ottava rima, but after Ariosto the next great master of the form was the English poet George Gordon, better known as Lord Byron. Byron's witty mind and gift of gab found ottava rima to be the perfect form for his *Don Juan*. The best-known modern practitioner of ottava rima is Kenneth Koch, who used it in his *Ko, or a Season on Earth* and *The Duplications*.

Some poets have used ottava rima for poems shorter than epics, but ottava rima is associated with long poems because its most

131

famous examples have been long: *Orlando Furioso* (38,736 lines) and *Don Juan* (15,784 lines). Like most epics, these poems are divided into cantos, the way a novel is usually divided into chapters. The first six lines of each stanza, rhyming *ababab,* seem to encourage the unwinding of the imagination, and the last two lines, rhyming *cc,* often give it a short pause to rest before continuing. It's a very comfortable form that allows the story to plunge straight ahead, digress, go off on a tangent, or switch to another thread of the plot, ranging freely through space and time. The best way to get a feel for ottava rima is to immerse yourself in reading it in great long stretches (without worrying too much about the parts you don't understand). Then get lots of paper and start writing a story that has the possibility of going on for a long time.

Pantoum
("pan-TOOM")

Pantoum is the Western word for the Malayan *pantun*, a poetic form that first appeared in the fifteenth century, in Malayan literature. It existed orally before then. Making up pantoums was highly popular, and Malayans knew the most famous ones by heart.

The Western version of the pantoum is a poem of indefinite length made up of stanzas whose four lines are repeated in a pattern: lines 2 and 4 of each stanza are repeated as lines 1 and 3 of the next stanza, and so on, as shown below:

_____ (Line 1)
_____ (Line 2)
_____ (Line 3)
_____ (Line 4)

_____ (Line 5 — same as line 2 above)
_____ (Line 6)
_____ (Line 7 — same as line 4 above)
_____ (Line 8)

_____ (Line 9 — same as line 6 above)
_____ (Line 10)
_____ (Line 11 — same as line 8 above)
_____ (Line 12)

And so on.

Sometimes the final stanza has a neat twist: although its first and third lines are as usual the same as the second and fourth lines in the stanza above it, its second and fourth lines are the same as the third and first lines of the very first stanza. This way, every line in the poem is used twice, and the first line of the poem is the same as the last. Rhyme is optional. It all sounds complicated, but if you look at

133

the example below, you'll see that our basic pantoum form is quite easy.

Because birds are gliding across your brain,
I rise into the shadows
And the mist is rolling in
Because my breath is rolling out.

I rise into the shadows
Like a pond that went to sleep:
Because my breath is rolling out
You hear doorbells in the woods.

Like a pond that went to sleep
And woke up inside a dream,
You hear doorbells in the woods
Though the woods are in the dream

And woke up inside a dream!
Although the air is filled with blue and white clouds,
Though the woods are in the dream,
A good idea can smell like pine trees.

Although the air is filled with blue and white clouds,
I am filled with ideas about dreams.
A good idea can smell like pine trees
And a dream can grow like a cloud.

I am filled with ideas about dreams.
The stars don't know what they mean
And a dream can grow like a cloud:
You can't explain this bigness.

The stars don't know what they mean
And the mist is rolling in.
You can't explain this bigness
Because birds are gliding across your brain.

The pantoum was first described in the West by Victor Hugo, poet and author of *The Hunchback of Notre Dame,* in 1829. Other French poets then wrote pantoums: Théodore de Banville, Louisa Siefert, Leconte de Lisle, Théophile Gautier, and, with considerable variation, Charles Baudelaire. The pantoum was taken up in England in the late nineteenth century, most notably by Austin Dobson in his "In Town" and James Brander Matthews in his "En Route."

The pantoum was used very little in America until it was revitalized by John Ashbery in his book *Some Trees* (1956); his "Pantoum," a variation on the basic pantoum form, inspired a group of young New York poets to write pantoums of their own and to teach pantoum writing to their students.

Part of the pleasure of the pantoum is the way its recurring lines gently and hypnotically twine in and out of one another, and the way they surprise us when they fit together in unexpected ways.

Parody
("PAHR-o-dee")

Parody is the exaggerated imitation, usually humorous, of a work or style of art. It is a type of satire, which makes fun of any and all human characteristics, not only the artistic. Parody is generally associated with literature and can be thought of as a form of criticism that approaches the subject from within. It works as a critical shorthand — a concrete rather than abstract method — and uses the thrusts of the original to reveal the vulnerability there, like a verbal kung fu.

Parody makes its points by using a serious style to express a somewhat ridiculous subject but is usually done in admiration, though sometimes in contempt.

Parody comes from the ancient Greek theater word *parodia*, meaning "a song sung beside," though its antecedents in humorous mimicry are doubtless prehuman. The Greek *parodia* was a satyr play following the main tragic dramas, performed by the same actors now dressed in grotesque costumes. It served the function of comic relief to the serious weight of tragedy. That form has persisted, loosely, through Shakespeare and into modern times — comic interludes or subplots, with their ludicrous parallels of the main doings.

The Greek philosopher Aristotle attributes the origin of formal parody to Hegemon of Thasos, who used epic style to represent people not as superior but inferior to what they are in real life. Others claim that the first parody was of Homer, "The Battle of the Frogs and the Mice." Aristophanes was the great parodist of ancient times, his masterpiece probably being *The Frogs,* ridiculing Greek tragedy.

During the Middle Ages parody concentrated on liturgy and other aspects of religious ritual. In the Renaissance, parodists tended to choose as their targets the classics and the new philosophic attitudes. The beginnings of the novel were awash with parody — Cervantes' *Don Quixote* a takeoff on knight-errantry, Fielding's *Shamela* derived from Samuel Richardson's novel of sentiment *Pamela*, Rabelais in *Gargantua and Pantagruel* poking wild fun at the Christian philosophy of his day.

English parody began in Miracle Plays and litany, but the first polished practitioner was Chaucer, particularly in "The Tale of Sir Thopas," which made fun of the grandiose medieval Romance.

European parody became regularized in the seventeenth century, as a weapon of debate, as a refreshment to hardening styles, and as just plain literary fun.

Wonderfully fine take-offs in the 1700s, such as Pope's mock epic "Rape of the Lock," were burlesque rather than true parody. The Golden Age of English parody was generally the Victorian Age, when inflated spiritual attitudes provided abundant fodder. Notable parodists were the Smith Bros. and, later in the nineteenth century, such masters of finesse as C.S. Calverly and J.K. Stephen. Lewis Carroll's works are loaded with parody, and Max Beerbohm was a perfectionist in parodic prose. James Joyce's great early twentieth-century works *Ulysses* and *Finnegans Wake* contain vast passages of parody.

In the nineteenth century, American parody featured such frontier-type figures as Mark Twain and Bret Harte, and in the twentieth perhaps surpassed the British in fineness with the New Yorker school — James Thurber, E.B. White, Robert Benchley, and S.J. Perelman.

Parody is strong today, this being a self-conscious, history-minded age. It is a parasitic art — and often conducted with malice — but ultimately as fundamental and necessary to literature as laughter is to mental well-being. Here is a parody of Robert Frost's poetry, by Firman Houghton.

Mr. Frost Goes South to Boston

When I see buildings in a town together,
Stretching all around to touch the sky,
I like to know that they come down again
And so I go around the block to see,
And, sure enough, there is the downward side.
I say to myself these buildings never quite
Arrived at heaven although they went that way.
That's the way with buildings and with people.
The same applies to colts and cats and chickens
And cattle of all breeds and dogs and horses.

I think the buildings Boston has are high
Enough. I like to ride the elevator
Up to the top and then back I come again.
Now, don't get me wrong. I wouldn't want
A ticket to New York to ride up higher.
These buildings come as close to heaven now
As I myself would ever want to go.

The initial "When I see" is taken from Frost's "Birches" (more than this should not be directly swiped). "Buildings in a town together" catches Frost's homely way of stating the obvious. The blank verse is nearly regular, touched with rural awkwardness, the language plain. Frost's poker-faced investigations of common sights are carried to ludicrousness in the image of the buildings' upward and downward sides. "That's the way" casts it into simple-minded philosophy, and the animal list exposes what may be at times a phony earthiness.

Readers familiar with the sentence structures of Henry James — long sentences garlanded with qualifying prepositional phrases, elegant and esoteric clauses, and a sort of higher slang ("flicked his cheek"), will enjoy the following by Max Beerbohm, the opening sentence of his Jamesian parody "The Guerdon":

> That it hardly was, that it all bleakly and unbeguilingly *wasn't* for "the likes" of *him*—poor decent Stanfordham—to rap out queries about the owner of the to him unknown and unsuggestive name that had, in these days, been thrust on him with such a wealth of commendatory gesture, was precisely what now, as he took, with his prepared list of New Year *colifichets* and whatever, his way to the great gaudy palace, fairly flicked his cheek with the sense of his having never before so let himself in, as he ruefully phrased it, without letting anything, by the same token, out.

Although both doing parodies and talking about literature are useful, parody can bring about a closer, more organic understanding of works of literature than any amount of critical talk.

Parody can be great fun. Many hilarious parodies are available and should be read aloud both for morale's and close knowledge's sake. It is helpful to read the original too if it is not widely familiar.

Read a bunch and analyze a few, noting the exact details of felicitous imitation and where the exaggeration and craziness come in.

Build a mood of joy. Good parody is a total, deep-down re-do, capturing and playing with the tone and subject of a work or an author or a style, not a minor alteration of surface features.

Parody's purpose, aside from laughter, is to reveal something of the soul of the original through re-creation and judicious askewness of its details.

Pastoral Poem

("PASS-tore-uhl")

Pastor is the Latin word for "shepherd." Pastoral poetry is poetry that depicts an often imaginary life in the country filled with happy characters who are shepherds, shepherdesses, and sometimes nymphs. The events and dialogues in traditional pastoral poems are not real but ideal.

The most famous examples of pastoral poetry are the Greek poet Theocritus's *Idyls* and the Latin poet Virgil's *Eclogues.* Other writers of pastoral poetry are Dante, Petrarch, Boccaccio, and Spenser, all of whom wrote what are called "eclogues."

An eclogue is a poem about rural life, usually in the form of a dialogue or monologue. Idyls are simply short pastoral poems in any form. Besides the eclogue and the idyl, varieties of pastoral poems include: the elegy (a lyric lamenting death); amoebaean poetry (verses spoken alternately by two speakers); and the *pastourelle* (a short narrative poem of the Middle Ages relating the random encounter of a knight and a shepherdess).

The term *pastoral poetry* is sometimes used more loosely to describe any poem that is written about country life, especially from the point of view of a city person thinking about the pleasures of the country.

In the sixteenth century, the English poet Christopher Marlowe began his well-known idyl "The Passionate Shepherd to His Love" this way:

> Come live with me and be my love,
> And we will all the pleasures prove
> That valleys, groves, hills, and fields,
> Woods or steepy mountain yields.

The last stanza of the poem gives a sense of the ideal or utopian concerns of the pastoral poem:

140

The shepherd's swains shall dance and sing
For thy delight each May morning
If these delights thy mind may move,
Then live with me and be my love.

Another sixteenth-century poet, Sir Walter Raleigh, answered
Marlowe's poem by writing "The Nymph's Reply to the Shepherd":

If all the world and love were young,
And truth in every shepherd's tongue,
These pretty pleasures might me move
To live with thee and be thy love.
[....]
But could youth last and love still breed,
Had joys no date nor age no need,
Then these delights my mind might move
To live with thee and be thy love.

Experiments in writing pastoral poetry can be made in a number
of ways. You can write a poem in any form about the pleasures and
perfection of living in the country. Or, you can create imaginary
rural characters who are having a dialogue about life and love. They
can be characters who exist in the present, past, or future. Another
possibility is to answer another poet's poem about rural life. This
gives you the chance to use objectivity and realism to confront the
traditional idealism of pastoral poetry, the way Raleigh answered
Marlowe by saying that youth is *not* eternal and the world is *not*
perfect. You could even write an "Ecological Eclogue."

See also: ECLOGUE.

Performance Poem

The performance poem is a poem written to be read or enacted in front of an audience. The poet can include other performance mediums, such as music, dance, theater, and video, to enhance or underscore the text.

Although the term "performance poetry" is relatively recent, poetry performances date back to ancient times. Much ancient poetry was intoned, chanted, or sung. The word *lyric* comes from "lyre," the stringed instrument of ancient Greece that accompanied the poem. In the eighth century B.C., Greek epics were composed for court recitation and entertainment. In the seventh century B.C., the choral lyric used as many as fifty voices. By the late sixth and fifth centuries B.C., Greek poetry was eclipsed by drama, which operated on a much grander scale, and was tied in with the seasonal ritual observances and the religious cult of Dionysus. The drama contained poetry, but the poetry was spoken by actors. The original lone poet, the lyric poet-singer, was enacting ritual as well, often to propitiate the gods, in order to make crops grow, or to cure various ills. The poet was of great spiritual and psychological importance to the community.

This is still true in certain cultures. (In Russia, thousands of people attend dramatic and passionate poetry readings and are moved to intense emotion.) The poet's role is related to the demanding role of the shaman (the "medicine" man or woman). The traditional tribal shaman worked with ritual chant and incantation to "travel" psychologically to other realms, to bring back wisdom to the community. The shaman's invocations were usually accompanied by the hypnotic repetition of a drumbeat, which would allow him or her to fall into a trance. In effect, the shaman was a conduit for the whole community, and it was through the gift of magical speech — or poetry — that the shaman communicated what was necessary. Thus poetry was required for understanding and expressing basic human needs, as well as honoring the sacredness of life.

Every culture has its epic poem that tells a story of the creation of the world, and chronicles the adventures of its gods and goddesses, heroes and heroines. Originally these epics were passed down orally through the generations. One thinks of communal situations now, such as around the campfire, with people singing together and telling stories, passing on traditional lore. Native Americans speak of "seeing the story in the flames." Try to imagine poetry in its origins, requiring an "audience."

Vachel Lindsay (1879-1931) certainly needed an audience on his tours: he went across America trading his poetry readings and drawings for room and board. A sort of populist showman of poetry, he gave chant-like readings of his own work, often accompanying himself on a drum.

Right around the First World War, the Dadaists, who were European experimental artists and poets, gave live spontaneous performances that often ended in confrontations with an outraged public or the police. The Dadaists, often wearing absurd costumes, performed their poems, songs, and stories, and for each of these there was an appropriate and unusual delivery. The Rumanian poet Tristan Tzara punctuated his poems with screams, sobs, and whistles. The German poet Richard Huelsenbeck accompanied his "Fantastic Prayers" by rhythmically swishing a riding crop through the air, or beating a large tom-tom. Like the tribal community with its shamans, the Dadaists were creating their work out of deep need, described by Hans (Jean) Arp:

> Revolted by the butchery of the 1914 World War, we in Zurich devoted ourselves to the arts. While the guns rumbled in the distance, we sang, painted, made collages and wrote poems with all our might. We were seeking an art based on fundamentals, to cure the madness of the age, and a new order of things that would restore the balance between heaven and hell.

The Italian and Russian Futurist poets also performed their work before startled audiences.

In recent times, the oral performance poem has been a good vehicle for poetry involved with social or political causes: civil rights, feminism, gay rights, and rallies against war, apartheid, and nuclear weapons. In these cases, the poet is speaking on behalf of a larger, often outraged community and, like the tribal shaman, envisions a better world.

The extremely varied Native American tradition has had a long and rich poetic history, based on shamanic rituals, continuing into the present with poets such as Peter Blue Cloud, Joy Harjo, and Simon Ortiz. Many Black American poets draw on their roots in African rituals, the drum beat, the blues, and jazz. The Black poets Amiri Baraka and Jayne Cortez perform their poetry with jazz musicians and vocalize their texts with great range and power.

Poets have been known to accompany themselves with alarm clocks, transistor radios, tape recorders, masks, strobe lights, stage "props," musical instruments, and special effects. The performance poet differs from the performance *artist* in that the poet is connected to a heritage of poetry, a maker and sounder of words.

The performance qualities of the following poem come alive only when it is read aloud, following the poet's instructions (given at the end of the poem).

skin

       Meat

              BONES   **(chant)**

I've come to tell you of the things dear to me
& what I've discovered of the skin

                Meat
                BONES

your body waking up so sweet to me   skin

dawn light it's green   skin

I'm in hungry repose
          Meat

it's getting close to motion   O skeleton
                 BONE

you might stretch it now   skin

so warm, flesh

and lasting awhile
       BONE

clock like a BONE creaking
memory like a BONE creaking

little laughter lines around the eyes   skin
& how the mouth's redder than the rest   Meat
or nipples off purple rib cage of
                BONES

It's morning anywhere!

O sitting and lying around in my weary tinsel skin
got to get up and walk around in my cumbersome skin
put on lightweight cotton skin
& shuffling skin slippers

the light's going to make it raw   skin
or vulnerable   Meat
or hard
        BONES

I could pierce it   skin
I'll grow new skin, undergo big character change

please get under my skin   take hold of me
interest or annoy me intensely

jump me out of my skin!

no skin off your nose, buster
he's thin-skinned, she's thick
dermis & epidermis mating

Allen's nephew once had a skin
                     head
                       haircut

O POOR FLAYED DEER WITH GENTLE HAIR

film on surface of milk this morning

only skin deep

let's go to the oily skin flick

TENDENCY OF HIGH FREQUENCY ALTERNATING CURRENT
TO FLOW THROUGH THE OUTER LAYER ONLY OF A CONDUCTOR

okay, you've wounded me, but it's only skin deep

I'm sitting down in my sweet smelling clammy skin
to eat some juicy MEAT!

145

one man's meat is another man's poison

animal flesh is tasty

HAD A DREAM THE MEAT WAS TURNED INSIDE OUT,
FLOWERS BLOOMING THERE

Had a dream the jackals came (this was in India)
to collect the Meat of my father's forefingers

O cloud shaped like a tenderloin steak

tree Meat

Meat of Buddha

Had a Meat sandwich   had a Meat day
everyone was carrying their Meat around, flinging
it in the breeze

Small town, downtown, spring: time to show off your Meat
go home when it's dark and sit down with the
                                        BONES

I live in a bare BONES room
he's working my fingers to the BONE
my friend Steven is living close to the BONE
I'm BONING up on my Dante, William Carlos Williams,
Campion and Gertrude Stein

Why is he such a bonehead? won't listen to a thing I say
Why are they so bone idle? won't do a thing I say
I'M GONNA POINT MY ABORIGINE BONE AT YOU & GET YOU WISER!

I've got a BONE to pick with the senator

I've got a BONE to pick with the Pentagon

The BONE of contention has to do with whether or not
we get a lease

Our old '68 Ford's an old BONE-shaker

Ivory, dentine, whalebone, dominoes, dice, castanets, corset
are some of the things made of BONE

but after I die make of my BONES, flutes
and of my skin, drums

I implore you in the name of all female deities wrathful &

                                                   compassionate

& PROTECT ENDANGERED SPECIES ALSO!

This piece is intended to be read aloud, singing the words "skin," "Meat," "BONES" as notes: "skin," high soprano register; "Meat," tenor; "BONES," basso profundo. The 3 notes may vary, but the different registers should be markedly distinguishable.

Before writing poems for performance it might be helpful to hear tapes or see films of poets reading or performing their work.

A good beginning exercise is to write a simple chant poem with repeating lines. You might then try reading your poem aloud in different ways, paying attention to the words, seeing where they guide the voice. Try working with singing, shouting, whispering. Then try having two people read the poem in unison, and then in alternating lines, then in a kind of round-robin overlapping pattern. Then have another person come in with a drum beat, again paying close attention to the rhythm and meaning of the text. It might be useful to tape record these experiments and play back the results.

The chant is only one possible type of performance poem. This genre is wide open for invention and play.

See also: CHANT, RAP POEM, RITUAL POEM.

Projective Verse

In 1950 the American poet Charles Olson published his essay "Projective Verse." In it, he describes a new kind of poetry, one that represents the poet's energy, and in which the poem acts as a field in which forces are at work. How the poem appears on the page is determined not by regular or "closed" forms (such as sonnets or rhyme and meter), but by forms that are "open," forms that allow for the pouring out of and replication of the poet's spirit on the page. How the poem appears on the page is an integral part of the meaning of the poem. The form is both an extension as well as a reflection of the poem's contents.

Projective verse is like a graph that shows how the poet writes the poem and how the poem should be read. Focusing on ideas of immediacy and spontaneity, Olson thought that the structure of the poem, the syntax and grammar, and the length of line might best be determined by the poet's individual rhythms, pauses, and breath.

The poet composes, according to Olson, not with some preconceived strategy, an already concluded idea of what to say. Rather, "one perception must immediately and directly lead to a further perception" (Edward Dahlberg, quoted by Olson), so the poet uses the act of writing to find out what the poem is going to say. In this way, the poem takes on an organic, living quality. As it is being written, it determines its own growth, develops its own demands for the writer and, eventually, the reader.

In the following poem by Gary Snyder we can see that how the poem appears on the page is related not only to how the poet has "breathed" it, but also to how the poet would like us to "breathe" and read it. The word placement and use of line show us how the poet would read it were he in the room with us. We would know where he'd breathe, where he'd stop, start, where the voice would accelerate or where it would slow down.

```
Burning the small dead
      branches
broke from beneath
   thick spreading
            whitebark pine.

            a hundred summers
snowmelt      rock      and air

hiss in a twisted bough.

   sierra granite;
            mt. Ritter
            black rock twice as old.

Deneb, Altair

windy fire
```

Note here how the spacing of the lines and words gives the poem a kind of crackling, quiet energy, the uneven sounds and sights of a fire. The long pause between "whitebark pine" and "a hundred summers" gives us a sense of the poet pausing, meditating on the world he is writing about. This same pause also gives us time to see the pine and branches. With the breaks between "snowmelt   rock   and air" we get a sense of the changing seasons of a century's summers in a real place.

You can write projective verse about anything. The more active your ideas and language, the more fun you can have with their arrangement and with communicating their energy in the poem.

Start your poem without really worrying about the lines and the structure. What you want to do is focus on letting the words fall on the page in the same way as they seem to be appearing to you. Are they coming in clusters? Then cluster them. Are they spinning out slowly, taking their time to appear? Then let them fall loosely and far apart. Try to let the poem determine its own direction, to let the images and ideas you write help lead you to the ones that follow.

When you've finished your poem, read it out loud. Does it sound the way you think it should? Where you want the reader to slow down—because as you wrote it you slowed down—have you shown the reader that this should happen? How would you have the poem speed up, make it as though riding on wind? Try varying the punctuation, the distances between words and between lines. How does doing this change the way you read the poem? How does it change its feel?

See also: FREE VERSE.

Prose Poem

As its name suggests, the prose poem is a cross between prose and poetry. It looks like prose but it reads like poetry without rhyme or a set rhythm. Often it has the imagery, density, quickness, and freshness of language that are associated with poetry. Prose poems tend to be short (from a couple of sentences to a couple of pages), but there are exceptions that run as long as fifty pages. Sometimes it is hard to distinguish between poetic prose and prose poetry (as in, for example, the writing of Gertrude Stein).

Aloysius Bertrand is credited with having invented the prose poem, in his *Gaspard of the Night* (1836). Bertrand influenced Charles Baudelaire's *Paris Spleen: Little Poems in Prose,* in which Baudelaire wrote:

> Which of us, in his ambitious moments, has not dreamed of the miracle of a poetic prose, musical, without rhyme and without rhythm, supple enough and rugged enough to adapt itself to the lyrical impulses of the soul, the undulations of the psyche, the prickings of consciousness?

Baudelaire in turn influenced the visionary poet Arthur Rimbaud.

Notable twentieth-century masters of the prose poem include Max Jacob, Pierre Reverdy, Luis Cernuda, Daniel Kharms, St.-Jean Perse, Jean Follain, Henri Michaux, Francis Ponge, and Julio Cortazar.

In the past thirty years, the prose poem seems to have been revived by American writers such as Russell Edson, David Ignatow, Robert Bly, James Wright, and W. S. Merwin. Many of these writers use impishness, surprise, incongruity, and humor in their work, as if they were playing hooky and enjoying it a lot. As Stuart Dybeck noted: "The short prose piece so frequently inhabits a No-Man's land between prose and poetry, narrative and lyric, story and fable, joke and meditation, fragment and whole," so that "part of the fun of

writing them is the sense of slipping between the seams." One of
Max Jacob's prose poems serves as a good example of this:

The Beggar Woman of Naples

When I lived in Naples, there was a beggar woman who sat at
the doorway of my building. I used to toss her a few coins before
getting into my carriage. One day, surprised at never being
thanked, I looked at the beggar woman. Now, as I looked, I saw
that what I had taken to be a beggar woman was a green,
wooden box containing some red dirt and a few half-rotten
bananas. . . .
    — *Translated by Ron Padgett*

You may find yourself writing a poem whose lines don't seem to
have any natural breaking points; try recopying it as prose. Or you
might find yourself trying to write a short story, when all you really
want to do is to capture a moment or series of moments; try leaving
out the characterization and plot. In both these cases, you can
rework your piece a little and perhaps turn it into a prose poem,
which might be the form it ought to have been in all along.

Quatrain
("KWOT-rain")

The quatrain is simply a poem or stanza of four lines. It is considered to be the favorite of the traditional English verse forms. The word *quatrain* comes from the French *quatre* and the Latin *quattuor*, both meaning "four."

A quatrain is often part of a longer poem that can be either rhymed or unrhymed. (If it is unrhymed, people call the quatrain a tetrastich, which literally means "to walk four.") If a quatrain is rhymed, the rhyme scheme could be *abab*, *abba*, *abcb*, or *aabb*.

The quatrain is the most common of all the stanza forms in European poetry and it is often used in songs, including traditional ballads. If we wonder why the quatrain has become such a popular form, part of the solution is in the meaning of the word *stanza*, which is what a quatrain also is. *Stanza* is an Italian word, originally meaning a stopping place, or a room. People like to have a regular pattern. They take pleasure in having an orderly way of stopping, resting, and then going on. In traditional poetry and in twentieth-century song, the quatrain provides this.

The eighteenth-century poet William Blake was famous for his mastery of the quatrain:

> Tyger! Tyger! burning bright
> In the forests of the night,
> What immortal hand or eye
> Could frame thy fearful symmetry?
> —From "The Tyger"

Here is another quatrain about animals by the twentieth-century poet T.S. Eliot:

> The hippopotamus's day
> Is passed in sleep; at night he hunts;
> God works in a mysterious way—
> The Church can sleep and feed at once.
> —From "The Hippopotamus"

153

Quatrains are self-contained and neat, unlike poetic forms that make you rush forward, like ottava rima. Try these two experiments: (1) think of all the poems and songs you know and see which are composed in quatrains; (2) try to write a poem or song in quatrains, so that its stanzas are both self-contained and interweaving with the whole, the way William Blake did:

The Tyger

Tyger! Tyger! burning bright
In the forests of the night,
What immortal hand or eye
Could frame thy fearful symmetry?

In what distant deeps or skies
Burnt the fire of thine eyes?
On what wings dare he aspire?
What the hand dare seize the fire?

And what shoulder, & what art,
Could twist the sinews of thy heart?
And when thy heart began to beat,
What dread hand? & what dread feet?

What the hammer? what the chain?
In what furnace was thy brain?
What the anvil? what dread grasp
Dare its deadly terrors clasp?

When the stars threw down their spears
And water'd heaven with their tears,
Did he smile his work to see?
Did he who made the Lamb make thee?

Tyger! Tyger! burning bright
In the forests of the night,
What immortal hand or eye
Dare frame thy fearful symmetry?

See also: STANZA, BALLAD, OTTAVA RIMA, COUPLET, TERCET.

Rap

R_{ap} is a Black English word that means "to talk," as in "I was rappin' to my girl the other day." Someone's "rap" is a presentation, spiel, or pitch that is meant to convince the listener that the ideas presented in the rap are valuable, and that the person presenting them is "cool."

Rap poetry is primarily an oral form — its power and beauty come from the sound and movement of the words working with or against a strong rhythmic background. Today rappers create that rhythm using an electronic background instead of tapping or clapping sounds. Sometimes "mouth music," a rhythmic beat created by making sucking, popping, and clicking sounds with the mouth and hands, is used as a background. A good regular rap has four accented beats per line and, performed aloud, runs to about 130 beats per minute. The tone of the rapper's voice and its modulation from loud to soft are also crucial to making rap work. Raps are usually stories about life in the city. They can be about street life, hard times, drugs, or personal relationships, and often take on an instructional tone.

Rap has its origins in the African oral traditions that travelled across to the Caribbean and the Old South. A form evolved there called "signifying," a sort of rhyming insult contest. In such verbal contests, the "Signifying Monkey" — a story form using the wily trickster character of the monkey who opposes bigger, stronger, but duller foes — is a basis of the rap form. The rapper is this Monkey-Warrior fighting his or her enemies with word magic.

The best way to write a rap is to start by listening to lots of music and rap poetry. Run DMC, Grandmaster Flash, and Kurtis Blow are good examples of current rap. Listen to them for hours on end, loud. At a certain point, your body will begin to become a musical instrument resonating with rap rhythms. Now you're ready. Think of a story you know well and start to tell it out loud to yourself or a friend using the rhythmic metre your body has been absorbing. If you have a tape recorder, record yourself and play it back. You'll hear yourself getting stuck on certain rhymes and tricky parts. They won't sound just right, or they'll sound too easy. Write the whole thing down and go over it again and again out loud so you can smooth it out.

Here's a rap poem by contemporary performance poet Bob Holman:

Rock'n'Roll Mythology

gotta ROCK'N'ROLL MYTHOLOGY
gotta total apocalpyse pathology
got the most PostHysterical Poetry
& if it ain't comin' at you then it's breezed on by

got the heavy duty political intent
got the worm farm free-form diamond noodle content
I got breezy ways & boppin' rays
when the word explodes the mother lode is where I'm at

& it's light here but you cannot see
doesn't matter anyway since you cannot breathe
you see the words mean, they're putting on the squeeze
that could strangle you — hey, what's that mean

say what he say
say what he say
he said he say
he said he said
say what he said
go on & say he said
what'd he say he said
that's what he said
that's what he said to say
he said to say

open up the book w/ yr finger hook
& scan it w/ yr television eyes
(televisionize televisionize televisionize televisionize)
you can stick it w/ yr eyes
stick out yr tongue & memorize
it's just you reading
the book is breathing
time's new dimension settles in

you are dancing on the edge of a thin thin dime
cause you are marching to the phone booth w/ a refugee line
you are baking in the kitchen when the walls cave
you are crawling through the desert w/ a loony rave
you are crossing all the x's for the love you save

hey who
hey who he
hey you
hey who you talkin' about, me?
hey listen to me, hey listen to me, hey listen to me, hey listen to me
hey listen to me, hey listen to me, hey listen to me, hey listen to me
I got to say what I say
to say what I see, I say
I don't see what you say
coming straight out of me
hey I'm coming straight out of you
why don't you try on that shoe
try it on for size
might give you a rise

cause everything I said it, I said it cause I read it
cause everything I said it, I said it cause I read it
& everything I said it, I said it cause I read it
& everything I said it, I said it cause I read it
& everything I said it, I said it cause I read it

gotta debunk all of those trashy ideals
gotta reintegrate all the ideas you steal
I understand means I stand under yr heel...

woowie, hey man, you gotta light
because really I think yr getting just a little bit too heavy.
well I realize that. why don't you give me a break & a half.
I could break yr arm. wouldn't do you any harm.
it's in the book, see. just take a look-see.
means what it says. says what it means.
it's only it. see what I mean.
I mean to say. there's nothing to it.
the book's overdue. so go renew it.

sing a song w/ a rock'n'roll band
play the guitar w/ a feather in yr hand

but the feather would rather fly than be plugged in
& the poetry just has to be freed from the pen

gotta gumbo anarchistic sensibility
& I do not exclude those who reject me
sail the manic Titanic awash in the wine-dark sea
where the language is the water & the rocks are poetry

gotta riptide w/ all hands going down
into hot pants where the love runs aground
gotta whamma jamma lamma w/ the low-down meltdown core
gotta relax the wax, Max, to de-rug the floor
gotta rocket in my pocket that can sock it more & more

& the central calmness of my Being is predicated quite simply
in the act of Seeing both within & without in a remarkable fashion
to which one must remark as a part of that act

gotta ROCK'N'ROLL MYTHOLOGY
gotta total apocalypse pathology
got the most PostHysterical Poetry
& if it ain't coming at you then it's breezed on by

got the heavy duty political intent
got the worm farm free-form diamond noodle content
I got breezy ways & boppin' rays
& when—hey, is that the end?
where it begins
ooo what a cheap shot
what a piece of cake shot

well. I suppose y'd rather leave it w/ a little downward trail
o, a demitasse of denouement to daily detail
not a bad idea in the kitchen making almond cakes & pies
what a pleasant surprise
go ahead & take a taste
one tiny slice
how nice

See also: PERFORMANCE POETRY.

Renga
("WREN-ga")

Renga are long, image-filled poems written in alternating stanzas of three lines and two lines, usually by a group of poets who take turns. In Japan, where renga originated as a party game, poets used to make renga of 1,000 or more stanzas, although 100 stanzas was the usual length. The great poet Matsuo Bashō (1644-1694) preferred renga of thirty-six stanzas, and this continues to be the popular length today.

Both haiku and senryu come from renga. A good renga combines the images and sensitivity to the natural seasons of haiku with the humor of senryu. Renga do not read like stories; each stanza "links" to the one before it, but not to the one before that. Writing renga allows poets to show off their skills at making images and seeing connections between seemingly unconnected things.

Renga began in Japan about a thousand years ago, where poets gathered for contests in writing the short poems called "tanka." When the contests were over they relaxed by writing poems together. These poems were like chained tanka, and could involve from two to two hundred poets in writing one poem.

Because writing renga was a game, the results were often thrown away after the game was over. But some poets wrote books of renga rules, including many examples of "hokku" or "starting verses" (see HAIKU) and of linking one stanza to another. They also talked about the pacing of a renga from beginning to middle to end.

Starting: The starting verse must include an image that suggests the season and place where the renga is being written.

Linking: There are many ways to connect, or "link" one stanza to another in renga. The most important ways involve writing down an image suggested by an image in the previous stanza, by making either a parallel image, a contrasting image, or a shift in focus onto another aspect of the same image.

Other ways to link stanzas include paying attention to the *words* of the previous stanza, by repeating prominent sounds or by making a pun, or play on words.

Finally, one can link a stanza simply by continuing or contrasting with the mood of the stanza before.

Pacing and Ending: The first six or eight stanzas of a renga are like the beginning of a party, when people introduce one another, a bit formally. In the middle twenty to twenty-four stanzas the party warms up, with stanzas that include humor and the whole range of human emotions. A renga ends with six or eight stanzas that move quickly through closely related images, with simple, straightforward linking, like the end of the party, when everyone gets ready to go home. Traditionally, the last stanza has a spring image, indicating hopefulness and peace.

Examples from Renga: The following groups of stanzas are taken from the beginning, middle, and end of different renga.

First are the opening six stanzas of "Cherry-Strewn Street." (Note that "cherry-strewn" refers to the petals of cherry blossoms.)

bringing home
a friend from afar
the cherry-strewn street

the white cat lazily blinks
the long afternoon

teacher's pet
cleaning the erasers
after school

thunder clouds
behind new leaves

after a shower
a sunbeam
on the garden stone

running out of the house
trailing the jump rope

> — *Tadashi Kondo, Kristine Young, Sherry Reniker,*
> *Robert Reed, Sachiko Karasawa, and Kazuyoshi Hirao*

New Jersey high school students included this sequence in one of their renga.

the corners of her mouth
trembling

the moon moves
the tide shifts
sand sinks into sand

the eclipse
a sliver of the sun

teeth marks in the pie
the dog
gets the rest

dentist's office
the sound of the drill

the oil well
pumping
in the barren field

> —*Susanne Hobson, Amy Ginnett, Karen Watson,*
> *Barbara Watson*

And here are the last six verses of "Ripe Cherry":

autumn haze
only a trickle of water
in the ditch

the adobe has faded
from pink to tan

she peels sunburnt skin
from his shoulders,
leaving white edges

under the bleached white bone
a grub

on the coyote fence
the first morning glory blossom
blue as sky

a single bee hums
in the morning stillness

> —*Elizabeth Searle Lamb, William J. Higginson,*
> *Penny Harter, and Richard Bodner*

The best way to get started with renga is to write haiku, then choose one as a starting verse. It also helps to read examples of renga, and try to see the connections that link one stanza to another.

Looking back at earlier stanzas can make it hard for you to move away from images that have already been used in the renga, but it may be a good idea, to make sure you do not fall into writing a story or connecting a series of images that all go together. The point of renga is to move around.

See also: HAIKU, SENRYU, TANKA.

Rhyme
("RIME")

Some scholars claim that rhyme was "invented" to help make stories memorable in the days before the printing press allowed writers to publish their stories. Rhyme was *not* invented, but is a phenomenon that results from our having only a limited number of sounds for making words. No human language is without rhyme.

What *was* invented before the printing press was a tradition of using meter and rhyme in regular patterns so that the story was memorable. This "bardic tradition" is alive and well today. Probably ninety-five percent of all popular songs written in the past ten years, like nearly all the songs written before we became "modern," rhyme exactly where tradition has decreed they should.

Many teachers discourage their students from writing rhymed poems. They point out that English vocabulary has relatively few words that rhyme, with the unhappy result that most rhymes have been "used up," and rhymed words in poems too often lead to clichés. If one reads the verses on commercial greeting cards, or analyzes most of the lyrics from popular songs, the banality of badly rhymed English sticks out like a razor blade in jello. Where one sees or hears the word "part," the next expected rhyme is "heart." If, perchance, the word is "soon," the reader may prepare for "moon."

This is not an inevitable situation. Poets like Sylvia Plath, whose work is widely anthologized, used rhyme in ways that challenge all this nay-saying. Manipulating sound is clearly one of the pleasures that allowed her to write such personal poems, and the word play creates a tension with the poems' subjects that makes for fascinating poetry. Songwriters such as Cole Porter and poets such as Kenward Elmslie seem to have a gift for clever rhyme, as shown in these lines from Elmslie's poem "Madonna's Milk Bar":

> I'm a member of the chorus
> Here at Hollywood and Vine.
> Who'd of thunk it. Punks adore us,
> Dig each funky monkeyshine.

All too often, people who use rhyme fail to recognize that the repetition of a sound should not automatically fall at the end of a line, on a "stressed" syllable. "Internal rhyme," where rhymes exist within the lines instead of at the ends, can create a unifying force within a poem, sometimes without the reader's noticing. "Burying" rhyme within a poem is a delightful way to honor the tradition/impulse of rhyming without battering it about the reader's head:

> I have waited long to see you
> As the seasons wait so patiently to change.
> And it's not strange that when you are here tonight
> There's something in my heart that's re-arranged.
> —From "Song for Townes Van Zandt"

In this song, poet Naomi Shihab Nye has mixed traditional rhyme schemes with the subliminal approach to repeating sounds. Nowhere in the song do we feel that normal speech patterns have been breeched in favor of rhyme, which is one of the greatest failings of rhyming poets. When the natural order of the words is rearranged to make possible an end rhyme, the device calls attention to itself in a particularly annoying way.

Slant rhyme (which has several other names) is the use of rhymes that are not perfect. "Breed" and "dread" is one example among thousands. *Feminine rhyme* is a rhyme (perfect or slant) between two words that end with unstressed syllables, as in "brother" and "mother." *Masculine rhyme* is the opposite: the rhymed sounds occur on stressed syllables, as in "behold" and "the gold." *Light rhyme* is the rhyming of a masculine-ending word with one that has a feminine ending.

A few words in English are thought to have no perfect, legitimate rhyme. These include: *orange, sugar, radio* and *elephant*. One of the best ways to build a list of rhyming words is to try to find words for which there is no rhyme. Make a list of every word you find that does rhyme with it, thus keeping it from the little list presented above. You might also take a look at a rhyming dictionary in the library.

See also: BOUT-RIMÉS.

Rhythm
("RITH-um")

Rhythm (or "measure") in writing is like the beat in music. In poetry, rhythm implies that certain words are produced more forcefully than others, and may be held for longer duration. The repetition of a pattern of such emphasis is what produces a "rhythmic effect." The word *rhythm* comes from the Greek, meaning "measured motion."

In speech, we use rhythm without consciously creating recognizable patterns. For example, almost every telephone conversation ends rhythmically, with the conversants understanding as much by rhythm as by the meaning of the words, that it is time to hang up. Frequently such conversations end with Conversant A uttering a five- or six-syllable line, followed by Conversant B's five to six syllables, followed by A's two- to four-syllable line, followed by B's two to four syllables, and so on until the receivers are cradled.

> Well I gotta go now.
> Okay, see you later.
> Sure, pal. So long.
> See you. Take care.
> Bye bye.
> Bye bye.

In poems, as in songs, a rhythm may be obvious or muted. A poem like Vachel Lindsay's "The Congo" consciously recreates the rhythms of a tribal dance:

> Fat black bucks in a wine-barrel room
> Barrel-house kings, with feet unstable,
> Sagged and reeled and pounded on the table,
> Pounded on the table,
> Beat an empty barrel with the handle of a broom,
> Hard as they were able

Boom, boom, BOOM,
With a silk umbrella and the handle of a broom,
Boomlay, boomlay, boomlay, BOOM.

On the other hand, some "free verse" has underlying rhythmical patterns that, while variable and not "regular" like Vachel Lindsay's, do nonetheless give a feeling of unity to the work. For example, read aloud the following lines a few times:

A chimney, breathing a little smoke.
The sun, I can't see
making a bit of pink
I can't quite see in the blue.
The pink of five tulips
at five P.M. on the day before March first.
— *From "February" by James Schuyler*

The most common units ("feet") of rhythm in English are:
- The *iamb*, consisting of two syllables, only the second accented (as in "good-bye").
- The *trochee*, two syllables, only the first accented (as in "awful").
- The *anapest*, three syllables, with only the third stressed (as in "Halloween").
- The *dactyl*, one stressed syllable followed by two unstressed (as in "wonderful").
- The *spondee*, two consecutive syllables that are both stressed (as in "big deal").

Many American poets in the past thirty years have written poetry using everyday language, and because much American speech is iambic in pattern, the poetry shows a lot of iambic rhythm. Learning something of other meters allows a writer to experiment with rhythmic variety, a poem's equivalent of musical syncopation. One good way to learn about rhythmic variation is to listen to bebop and modern jazz, and to dance. Rhythm is a skill that is best learned through the ears and legs, not through the brain.

See also: FOOT, LINE, PROJECTIVE VERSE.

Ritual Poem

People have always needed to feel that they had *some* control over the powerful forces that shaped their lives — particularly the forces of nature. One way they tried to assert this control was by performing rituals.

Rituals are ceremonies enacted for the spirits or gods who, it was and is believed, direct man's fate. The ceremonies were meant to persuade the spirits to turn fate in one direction or the other: to bring rain or sun, to stop storms, to provide protection from fire and flood, to bring healthy babies. Before hunting, rituals were performed to lure forth whatever animal was being hunted. Before battle, they were performed to insure victory. Often the rituals included singing, dancing, and eating.

The person who decided what each ritual should be was called a *shaman*. The shaman was the spiritual leader of the community. The first poets are thought to have been shamans, so ritual poems are among the oldest forms of poetry. There are many types of ritual poems and there is no single set of rules for all of them. One type includes a series of directions for doing something to get the attention of the spirits. For example, in "Storm Ritual," Alaskan Eskimos were trying to persuade the spirits to make a storm subside — and to persuade themselves that they could overcome it.

Storm Ritual
1. Build a snowman with a big head.
2. Give the snowman's head a large mouth.
3. Catch salmon, skin the carcasses, freeze them.
4. Hack away at the frozen fish and push the pieces into the snowman's mouth.
5. Afterward, have a big feast in which all the pieces of fish are eaten.

A more contemporary ritual poem comes from the Kwakiutl Indians, who live in northwestern Canada. The ritual poem was thought to bestow good luck on a newborn child.

Gift Ritual
1. Start by giving away different glass bowls.
2. Have everyone give everyone else a glass bowl.
3. Give away handkerchiefs and soap.
4. Give away a sack of clams.
5. Give away pigs and geese and chickens, or pretend to do so.
6. Pretend to talk Chinese and give away something.
7. Make a narrow place at the entrance of a house and put a line across it that you have to stoop under to get in.
8. Hang the line with all sorts of pots and pans that make a big noise.
9. Give away these pans while saying things like "Here is a pan worth $100, and here's one worth $200."
10. Give everyone a new name.
11. Give the newborn child a name.

Inspired by a recent eclipse, a student wrote this ritual poem:

Eclipse Ritual
1. Turn off the lights and give paper moons to everyone.
2. Pretend your face is the sun and put the moon in front of it.
3. Say DARK DARK DARK DARK and close your eyes.
4. Say ECLIPSE ECLIPSE ECLIPSE ECLIPSE.
5. Then become one by wearing dark clothes.

Here are some things to remember when writing this type of ritual poem:

1. Decide what you would like to have occur.
2. Examine all aspects of the subject.
3. Think of actions to illustrate some of these aspects.
4. Write each action down as a command.
5. Number the commands.
6. Let yourself go.

Another type of ritual poem mentions sacred places and objects in a way that confirms the tribe's belief in the rightness of everything, as in this ritual poem for girls' puberty rites that help the girls "[stand] up for their dance in the way of life":

Songs of the Masked Dancers

1
When the earth was made
when the sky was made
when my songs were first heard
the holy mountain was standing toward me with life.

At the center of the sky, the holy boy walks four ways with life.
My mountain became my own: standing toward me with life.
The dancers became: standing toward me with life.

When the sun goes down to the earth
where Mescal Mountain lies with its head toward the sunrise
black spruce became: standing up with me.

2
Right at the center of the sky the holy boy with life walks in
      four directions.
Lightning with life in four colors comes down four times.
The place called black spot with life,
the place called blue spot with life,
the place called yellow spot with life,
they have heard about me
the black dancers dance in four places.
The sun starts down toward the earth.

3
The living sky black-spotted
The living sky blue-spotted
The living sky yellow-spotted
The living sky white-spotted
The young spruce as girls stood up for their dance in the way
      of life.

When my songs first were, they made my songs with words of
      jet.
Earth when it was made
Sky when it was made
Earth to the end
Sky to the end
Black dancer, black thunder, when they came toward each other

All the bad things that used to be vanished.
The bad wishes that were in the world all vanished.
The lightning, the black thunder struck four times for them.
It struck four times for me.

4
When my songs first became
when the sky was made
when the earth was made
the breath of the dancers against me made only of down:
when they heard about my life
where they got their life
when they heard about me:
it stands.
    — *Traditional*

On a more everyday level, we all follow our own little rituals, in
the particular way we brush our teeth, visit our grandparents, say
goodbye, and so on, and there is no reason why good poems can't be
written about these rituals as well.

See also: CHANT, EVENT POEM.

Rondeau
("ron-DOE")

The French word *rondeau* comes from the French *rond*, meaning "round." Most everyone has sung a round such as "Row, Row, Row Your Boat" at one time or another. In this poem the repeating lines as well as the rhyming sounds give the poem the quality of a round, and most likely this form, like many poetic forms from the past, was originally sung.

The rondeau is one of the French fixed forms, related to the earlier rondel and the triolet. In fact, all three are variations of the same genre, and the rondel and rondeau have, at times, been synonymous.

Around 1500, the rondeau form became fixed as a thirteen-line poem, with lines of eight or ten syllables each, divided into stanzas of five, three, and five lines. The whole poem is constructed around two rhymes, and the first words (or sometimes the whole first line) are used as a refrain that repeats, independent of the rhyme scheme, at the end of the second and third stanzas (adding two lines to the basic thirteen). If R stands for the refrain, the scheme of the rondeau looks like this:

Stanza 1: *A (R)*
A
B
B
A

Stanza 2: *A*
A
B
(R)

Stanza 3: *A*
A
B
B
A
(R)

The following rondeau is by a French poet named Vaillant who lived in the fifteenth century. It is about losing a girlfriend to someone else. (This is a loose translation, attempting to keep the sense and flavor of the poem, at the same time changing the end words in order to maintain the rhyme scheme. For example, in French, *dame* means "lady" rather than "girl," but the translator's idea was to use an end-word that more or less rhymes with "soul.")

A(R)	Listen, everyone! I have lost my girl
A	For he who finds her, on my soul
B	Even though she is fair and kindly
B	I give her up heartily
A	Withough raising a stink at all
A	This girl knows her graces well
A	God knows, she loves and is loyal
B	For heaven's sake, let him keep her secretly
R	Listen, everyone! I have lost my girl
A	Look after her well, this pearl
A	Let no one hurt or wound her
B	For by heaven, this pretty
B	Is sweetness itself to everybody
A	Woe is me! I cry to the world
R	Listen, everyone! I have lost my girl.

The following modern rondel was written by Frank O'Hara (1926-1966). It is a twelve-line form with three stanzas and one floating line (line 9) and adheres to the form by its opening repeating line. Rhyme and strict syllabic count have been abandoned. This poem is delightful, fantastical, and puzzling. The "things" in the poem — cigars, covers, rose, nugget, and flies — seem to have no relationship to one another except through the occasion of the poem. The repeating line "Door of America, mention my fear to the cigars!" is wonderfully mysterious, and an odd command.

Rondel

Door of America, mention my fear to the cigars!
dance the ch' Indian and quit the covers;
the cigars owe you for toy-chanting to them,
joke used up, having petty symbols.

Lake roses, surrounding the plural natal mates,
eat the nugget of blank fate and then drop the
door of America. Mention my fear to the cigars!

Plural moments are trapped by the passing ravishments.

The Muse becomes a comrade who poses for you
when you are bivouacked and want to get out of the aura:
set rhythms quit, vapid, and flies grow pale.
Door of America, mention my fear to the cigars!

Traditionally the rondeau is a light and playful form, often with a philosophical tone, as in the Vaillant poem. The attitude seems to be something like this: "In spite of lost love, I can still sing," or "In spite of cold winter, the spring is coming." It might be interesting to take a subject that is irritating, and to challenge it through the poem. For example, one might turn a complaint into a good-humoured affirmation. Or if you are more interested in particular random words or a tone, you can make up a wild opening line like Frank O'Hara's and "wing it," letting the mind free-associate and ramble.

See also: TRIOLET.

Satire
["SA(T)-tire"]

The word *satire* probably comes from the Latin *satura* and refers to a "medley" of verse. Some scholars believe that the word comes from the Greek *satyros*, meaning satyr, those crude, rude, and lewd creatures of myth who used their powers to expose people's faults and ridicule them without mercy. Today satire is not a poetic form that can be described in terms of meter, rhyme, or stanza length. It is, rather, a tone or point of view the writer takes when writing a piece that is both critical and mocking. The object of attack can be a person, an institution, or an idea. However, satire is not a frontal attack. It does not take the moral high-ground of a self-righteous assault; it makes its point through humor and wit, like *Mad* magazine.

When you are made to laugh *at* someone, your awe for that person is diminished, and that person then has less power over you. A lot of people laughing in a thoughtful and illuminated way can result in social or moral change. Good satirists want more than simply to complain about something. They hope to provoke thought and change through humor and wit.

Mocking the thing you don't like goes back a long way and has roots in many cultures. Most of the satyrical poems of Archilochos (probably seventh century B.C.) have been lost, but we can read the very funny satirical plays of Aristophanes (448-380 B.C.).

Roman satirical authors include Lucilius (180-102 B.C.), who made satire popular in Rome; Horace, the most famous Roman satirist; and Juvenal, Martial, Petronius, Apuleius, and Lucian.

Outstanding English satirists in poetry are John Skelton, Ben Jonson, John Dryden, and Alexander Pope, and in prose Jonathan Swift and Henry Fielding.

Although the best-known contemporary satirists are in cartoons (*Mad* magazine), in stand-up comedy (Lenny Bruce and Mort Sahl), and in journalism (Art Buchwald and Russell Baker), there have been

some good satirical poems in the past couple of decades, such as
Gregory Corso's "Marriage":

Marriage
for Mr. and Mrs. Mike Goldberg

Should I get married? Should I be good?
Astound the girl next door
with my velvet suit and faustus hood?
Don't take her to movies but to cemeteries
tell all about werewolf bathtubs and forked clarinets
then desire her and kiss her and all the preliminaries
and she going just so far and I understanding why
not getting angry saying You must feel! It's beautiful to feel!
Instead take her in my arms
lean against an old crooked tombstone
and woo her the entire night the constellations in the sky—

When she introduces me to her parents
back straightened, hair finally combed, strangled by a tie,
should I sit knees together on their 3rd-degree sofa
and not ask Where's the bathroom?
How else to feel other than I am,
a young man who often thinks Flash Gordon soap—
O how terrible it must be for a young man
seated before a family and the family thinking
We never saw him before! He wants our Mary Lou!
After tea and homemade cookies they ask What do you do?
Should I tell them? Would they like me then?
Say All right get married, we're losing a daughter
but we're gaining a son—
And should I then ask Where's the bathroom?
O God, and the wedding! All her family and her friends
and only a handful of mine all scroungy and bearded
just waiting to get at the drinks and food—
And the priest! he looking at me as if I masturbated
asking me Do you take this woman
for your lawful wedded wife?
And I, trembling what to say, say Pie Glue!
I kiss the bride all those corny men slapping me on the back:
She's all yours, boy! Ha-ha-ha!
And in their eyes you could see

175

some obscene honeymoon going on—
Then all that absurd rice and clanky cans and shoes
Niagara Falls! Hordes of us! Husbands! Wives! Flowers!
All streaming into cozy hotels
All going to do the same thing tonight
The indifferent clerk he knowing what was going to happen
The lobby zombies they knowing what
The whistling elevator man he knowing
The winking bellboy knowing
Everybody knows! I'd be almost inclined not to do anything!
Stay up all night! Stare that hotel clerk in the eye!
Screaming: I deny honeymoon! I deny honeymoon!
running rampant into those almost climactic suites
yelling Radio belly! Cat shovel!
O I'd live in Niagara forever! in a dark cave beneath the Falls
I'd sit there the Mad Honeymooner
devising ways to break marriages, a scourge of bigamy
a saint of divorce—

But I should get married I should be good
How nice it'd be to come to her
and sit by the fireplace and she in the kitchen
aproned young and lovely wanting my baby
and so happy about me she burns the roast beef
and comes crying to me and I get up from my big papa chair
saying Christmas teeth! Radiant brains! Apple deaf!
God what a husband I'd make! Yes, I should get married!
So much to do! like sneaking into Mr. Jones' house late at night
and cover his golf clubs with 1920 Norwegian books
Like hanging a picture of Rimbaud on the lawnmower
Like pasting Tannu Tuva postage stamps
all over the picket fence
Like when Mrs. Kindhead comes to collect
for the Community Chest
grab her and tell her There are unfavorable omens in the sky!
And when the mayor comes to get my vote tell him
When are you going to stop people killing whales!
And when the milkman comes leave him a note in the bottle
Penguin dust, bring me penguin dust, I want penguin dust—

Yet if I should get married and it's Connecticut and snow
and she gives birth to a child and I am sleepless, worn,
up for nights, head bowed against a quiet window,

176

the past behind me,
finding myself in the most common of situations
a trembling man
knowledged with responsibility not twig-smear
nor Roman coin soup—
O what would that be like!
Surely I'd give it for a nipple a rubber Tacitus
For a rattle a bag of broken Bach records
Tack Della Francesca all over its crib
Sew the Greek alphabet on its bib
And build for its playpen a roofless Parthenon—
No, I doubt I'd be that kind of father
not rural not snow no quiet window
but hot smelly tight New York City
seven flights up, roaches and rats in the walls
a fat Reichian wife screeching over potatoes Get a job!
And five nose-running brats in love with Batman
And the neighbors all toothless and dry haired
like those hag masses of the 18th century
all wanting to come in and watch TV
The landlord wants his rent
Grocery store Blue Cross Gas & Electric Knights of Columbus
Impossible to lie back and dream Telephone snow,
ghost parking—
No! I should not get married I should never get married!

But — imagine if I were married to a beautiful
sophisticated woman
tall and pale wearing an elegant black dress
and long black gloves
holding a cigarette holder in one hand
and a highball in the other
and we lived high up in a penthouse with a huge window
from which we could see all of New York
and even farther on clearer days
No, can't imagine myself married to that pleasant prison dream—

O but what about love? I forget love
not that I am incapable of love
it's just that I see love as odd as wearing shoes—
I never wanted to marry a girl who was like my mother
And Ingrid Bergman was always impossible
And there's maybe a girl now but she's already married

177

And I don't like men and—
but there's got to be somebody!
Because what if I'm 60 years old and not married,
all alone in a furnished room with pee stains on my underwear
and everybody else is married! All the universe married but me!

Ah, yet well I know that were a woman possible
as I am possible
then marriage would be possible—
Like SHE in her lonely alien gaud waiting her Egyptian lover
so I wait — bereft of 2,000 years and the bath of life.

The best way to learn to write satire is to read it, lots of it, to get its "feel." Then, when you decide what you're going to satirize, aim your humor at specific details. Let's say you want to write a poem satirizing the way the President is doing his or her job. It's not enough to feel vaguely dissatisfied. You must aim your barbs at specific things the President does and the way they're done. (Criticizing the President because he has a funny-looking nose is not satire, it's caricature.) One test that may help you know if your satire is working is if you laugh while you're writing it.

Senryu
(Sounds like "SEND-you" with an *r* instead of a *d*)

Senryu has the same form and origin as the haiku, but there are differences. While the haiku poet tries to capture a keenly perceived moment in which nature is linked to human nature, the senryu poet aims directly at human nature. Also, the language of senryu is direct and to the point, sometimes sarcastic, always humorous.

Like haiku, senryu grew out of renga. Without bothering to compose full renga, people began playing a game of "can you top this," adding one renga stanza to another. This game almost always produced funny verses, short, humorous stanzas in haiku form: senryu.

Here are some examples (the first three are translated from the Japanese by William J. Higginson).

crazy for me,
she was, I find out
fifty years later
—*Kenkabō*

the cheap kite
flying only when
he runs with it
—*Anonymous*

looking for the shoes
of the visitor—the little boy
has them on
—*Kōka*

Her name forgotten...
the sweetheart my father said
I would forget
—*Ross Kremer*

squinting
  to read the sign
   "optician"
      —*Alan Pizzarelli*

Before giving me
  her garden's peony
   my neighbor thinks twice
      —*Sydell Rosenberg*

Senryu require the same sort of concentration that you must give to haiku. If you look through a group of haiku you have written, the chances are that some of them *are* senryu.

See also: HAIKU, RENGA, TANKA.

Sestina
("sess-TEE-na")

To remember this delightful form, it helps to know that the word *sestina* comes from the Latin *sextus*, which means "sixth." This form is based on sixes and it seems like the ideal writing experiment for a mathematical mind.

The sestina has six unrhymed stanzas of six lines each in which the words at the ends of the first stanza's lines recur in a rolling pattern at the ends of all the other lines. The sestina then concludes with a tercet (three-line stanza) that also uses all six end-words, two to a line. In the diagram of the sestina form below, the letters *A-F* stand for the six end-words of the sestina:

Stanza 1: *A*
         B
         C
         D
         E
         F

Stanza 2: *F*
         A
         E
         B
         D
         C

Stanza 3: *C*
F
D
A
B
E

Stanza 4: *E*
C
B
F
A
D

Stanza 5: *D*
E
A
C
F
B

Stanza 6: *B*
D
F
E
C
A

Tercet: *AB*
CD
EF

It's easier to understand the pattern by looking at an example, such as the following sestina by American poet Elizabeth Bishop, which has six simple end-words:

A: house
B: grandmother
C: child
D: stove
E: almanac
F: tears.

Sestina

September rain falls on the house.
In the failing light, the old grandmother
sits in the kitchen with the child
beside the Little Marvel Stove,
reading the jokes from the almanac,
laughing and talking to hide her tears.

She thinks that her equinoctial tears
and the rain that beats on the roof of the house
were both foretold by the almanac,
but only known to a grandmother.
The iron kettle sings on the stove.
She cuts some bread and says to the child,

It's time for tea now; but the child
is watching the teakettle's small hard tears
dance like mad on the hot black stove,
the way the rain must dance on the house.
Tidying up, the old grandmother
hangs up the clever almanac

on its string. Bird-like, the almanac
hovers half open above the child,
hovers above the old grandmother
and her teacup full of dark brown tears.
She shivers and says she thinks the house
feels chilly, and puts more wood in the stove.

It was to be, says the Marvel Stove.
I know what I know, says the almanac.
With crayons the child draws a rigid house
and a winding pathway. Then the child
puts in a man with buttons like tears
and shows it proudly to the grandmother.

But secretly, while the grandmother
busies herself about the stove,
the little moons fall down like tears
from between the pages of the almanac
into the flower bed the child
has carefully placed in the front of the house.

Time to plant tears, says the almanac.
The grandmother sings to the marvellous stove
and the child draws another inscrutable house.

Now read the poem aloud and notice how it builds on the end-words, and how their emphasis shifts in the changing grammar of the poem, and how one never tires of these words. The whole poem has a hypnotically rhythmic quality, like the rain it evokes. It's also interesting to track one of the words, such as *tears,* and feel its nuances: "hide her tears," "equinoctial tears," "small hard tears," "dark brown tears," "buttons like tears," "moons fall down like tears," and "Time to plant tears."

Notice also how the pattern works. The order of the end-words is derived from each previous stanza. For example, the *first* end-word of stanza 2 is that of the *last* end-word of stanza 1, the second end-word of stanza 2 is that of the first end-word of stanza 1, the third end-word of stanza 2 is that of the second-to-last end-word of stanza 1, and so on.

Likewise, the end-words of stanza 3 follow the same "windshield wiper" method of bringing them down from stanza 2, and so on. Note that in the tercet (at the end of the poem) three of the end-words appear in the middle of the lines and three at the ends, but if you check their order — presto — it's back to *ABCDEF.* Actually, many poets (such as Elizabeth Bishop) arrange the tercet end-words in any order they want, but the classical pattern ends up with *ABCDEF.*

The sestina is said to have been invented by the troubadour poet Arnaut Daniel. It was widely used by his followers, as well as by Dante and Petrarch in Italy. The word *troubadour* comes from the Provençal word *trobar,* meaning "to find," or "to invent in verse." The troubadours were travelling French poet-musicians, some of them noblemen or crusader-knights, who flourished from the end of the eleventh century through the thirteenth century.

Appearing here and there through the ages (as in Sir Philip Sidney's double sestina in the sixteenth century), the sestina seems to have revived in recent history. Ezra Pound and W.H. Auden both enjoyed composing in this form, and many contemporary poets have written sestinas. One by John Ashbery features Popeye.

To write a sestina, you might begin by picking six end-words, perhaps words that suggest physical substance (such as *chair* or *mountain*). Then write a first verse using all six end-words and see what comes up. At that point, you might want to write down all the other end-words, in correct rotation, way over on the right-hand side of the page, so you won't have to worry about it in the middle of writing the rest of the poem.

In other sestinas, you might want to vary the types of the end-words, using, say, two nouns, an adjective, a verb, a conjunction, and an interjection. It's interesting how almost any six words, used in a sestina, will tend to generate a scene or little story.

Skeltonic Verse
("skell-TAHN-ic")

Skeltonic verse is the name of a poetic form of short lines (averaging from three to six words) whose rhymes are continued as long as the poet feels it's working well. The fast and frequent rhyming becomes the main structural feature of this poetry. It is also called "tumbling verse" because of the way the lines tumble out of the poet's brain like a bag of drumsticks poured onto a basketball court. Because the lines are so short and because the lists of end rhymes can go on as long as the poet likes, there is a playfulness and heavy-handed rhythm to this form that makes it a lot of fun to work with.

Skeltonic verse was named after its inventor, the English poet John Skelton (ca. 1460-1529). He had used many of the elaborate poetic forms of his time, but began to feel they were getting dull and unable to convey the pulse of life in the English language as people were speaking it. So he started writing in short, spontaneous lines where his thoughts and feelings did not have to be stretched to fit fancier poetic forms. The skeltonic may seem simple and crude, but it is a great vehicle for conveying energetic feeling with humor.

To write a skeltonic, pick a subject you feel strongly about and let the rhymes carry the poem along, beginning a new group of rhymes when the last group seems to be losing its punch (Skelton's groups are between two and five rhymes long).

Here are two examples of the skeltonic; the first is part of a long poem by Skelton himself, and the second a section from a recent attempt at the form by Allen Ginsberg.

> What can it avail
> To drive forth a snail,
> Or to make a sail
> Of an herring's tail?
> To rhyme or to rail,
> To write or to indict,
> Either for delight

186

Or else for despite?
Or bookes to compile
Of divers manner style,
Vice to revile
And sin to exile?
To teach or to preach,
As reason will reach?
Say this, and say that,
His head is so fat,
He wotteth never what
Nor whereof he speaketh;
He crieth and he creaketh,
He prieth and he peeketh,
He chides and he chatters,
He prates and he patters,
He clitters and he clatters,
He meddles and he smatters,
He gloses and he flatters;
Or if he speak plain,
Then he lacketh brain,
He is but a fool;
Let him go to school,
On a three-footed stool
[...]
   And if ye stand in doubt
Who brought this rhyme about,
My name is Colin Clout.

        —From "Colin Clout"

Sincerity
is the key
to living
in Eternity

If you love
Heav'n above
Hold your ground,
Look around
Hear the sound
of television,

No derision,
Smell your blood
taste your good
bagels & lox
Wash your sox
& touch wood,
It's understood
This is it
wild wit
Make your love
on earth above,
home of the brave,
Save yr grave
for future days
Present here
nothing to fear
No need to sigh
no need to die
before your time
mentally whine
stupidly dine
on your own meat
That's what's neat
Mortally great
Immortally sweet
Incredibly deep
makes you weep
Just this once
Don't be a dunce
Take your cap
off Hear my rap

Sincerity
is the key
to living in
Eternity
            —*From "Jumping the Gun on the Sun"*

Sonnet
("SAH-net")

A sonnet is a fourteen-line poem, thought to have been invented around the year 1200 by the poet Giacomo da Lentino (ca. 1200-1250). It is one of the most well known of all the verse forms in the Western world. The word *sonnet* is derived from the Italian word *sonetto*, a little sound or song, which came from the Latin *sonus*, meaning "a sound."

The sonnet form involves a certain way of thinking: the setting up or development of a thought or idea which is brought to a conclusion at the end of the poem. Sticking to one subject in the sonnet and creating pauses at the ends or in the middles of lines make the poem resemble the way we think when we are thinking about a single idea.

The most well-known sonnets are by Petrarch, Spenser, Shakespeare, Milton, and Wordsworth. Other great writers of sonnets include Elizabeth Barrett Browning, Thomas Wyatt, W.H. Auden, Rainer Maria Rilke, Edna St. Vincent Millay, Dante, Gerard Manley Hopkins, and Dylan Thomas.

The most common form of the sonnet is a fourteen-line poem in two parts: an octave (eight lines) and a sestet (six lines). The octave can be divided into two four-line stanzas and the sestet can be divided into one four-line stanza and a couplet (the two lines at the end). The chance to have two lines at the end, set off from the rest of the poem, often gives the poet the moment to conclude the poem's thought in a momentous and satisfying way.

In terms of sound and rhyme, there are many different ways of writing a sonnet. Many traditional sonnets were written in the meter of iambic pentameter, in which there are five feet or ten syllables to every line and every other syllable is accented:

> When to the sessions of sweet silent thought
> I summon up remembrance of things past,
> I sigh the lack of many a thing I sought,
> And with old woes new wail my dear Time's waste.

Then can I drown an eye, unused to flow,
For precious friends hid in death's dateless night,
And weep afresh love's long since canceled woe,
And moan th' expense of many a vanished sight;
Then can I grieve at grievances foregone,
And heavily from woe to woe tell o'er
The sad account of fore-bemoaned moan,
Which I new pay as if not paid before,
    But if the while I think on thee, dear friend,
    All losses are restored and sorrows end.
      —*Shakespeare, "Sonnet 30"*

    Traditional rhyme schemes for the sonnet vary a lot, the most famous being *abab, cdcd, efef, gg* (Shakespeare), but Wordsworth often did it this way: *abbaaccb, dedeff.* The rhymes and sound schemes of the sonnet are similar to those of the ballad and of popular songs, but the sonnet is not a narrative poem and is usually more complex or condensed, and more contained within itself, since it is shorter and has no repetition of lines or refrain.

    Nowadays it is possible to write sonnets that have no particular meter or rhyming schemes. The best way to write them is to read a lot of sonnets by other writers and then write a fourteen-line poem that encompasses the method of thought that the sonnet gives room for.

    Here is an example of a modern sonnet:

Each tree stands alone in stillness
After many years still nothing
The wind's wish is the tree's demand
The tree stands still
The wind walks up and down
Scanning the long selves of the shore
Her aimlessness is the pulse of the tree
It beats in tiny blots
Its patternless pattern of excitement
Letters birds beggars books
There is no such thing as a breakdown
The tree the ground the wind these are
Dear, be the tree your sleep awaits
Sensual, solid, still, swaying alone in the wind
      —*Ted Berrigan, "Sonnet XVII"*

Though sonnets can be written about any subject, they seem very often to be written about love and/or philosophy. This is because, as each poetic form reflects a human way of thinking, the sonnet form seems to reflect the way people think about ideas of love. Maybe that's why there is the need for a conclusion—as if we could attempt, through poetry, to make sense of our feelings about love, or to say something final and sublime about a particular thought about love, even just for the moment.

Therefore, if you want to write in the sonnet form, it's good to understand the concept of "therefore." The octave presents the situation you and/or the world are in (describe it in eight lines; it can be two stanzas or one). In the sestet of the sonnet, what the poet is doing is saying, "Therefore, I feel this way about it all. . . ." You can race to a conclusion in six lines or you can write in a meditative way for four lines, then pause and create a couplet at the end which winds up being your ultimate statement on the situation described in the octave.

You don't have to worry about meter and rhyme until you've gotten accustomed to the method of thought that is reflected in the sonnet. After you write three or four sonnets, you can begin to experiment with making the sonnet sound like a song that has rhymes and a beat, if you want to.

Besides writing about love, you can write sonnets about things that happen when you're walking down the street or any thing or idea you want to describe (octave), and then, what you think of that (sestet).

Many literary critics thought Wordsworth and Hopkins took liberties with the sonnet form—you should feel free to take them too.

Some poets have written groups of sonnets that are connected with each other. These are called sonnet cycles or crowns or garlands of sonnets.

See also: STANZA, QUATRAIN, COUPLET.

Spoonerism

Named after W.A. Spooner (1844-1930), an Englishman who was a known botcher of words, a spoonerism is the swapping of the initial sounds of two words to create two different words, as in "word botcher" (from "bird watcher.")

A list of spoonerisms might be longer than you think. Consider the number of words that rhyme and realize that any two words that have rhymes are candidates for spoonerization, since all spoonerised words rhyme with the two words from which they have been spoonerised. A *great day* would be a *gray date*. The *right time* would be a *tight rhyme*. A character named Lew Tate might never arrive on time, unlike Sue Toon.

If you develop the habit of playing with language, hunting for spoonerisms may become a natural extension of your thinking process. As words are spoken, you are thinking "spurreds are woken," making a special list of those that convert into especially interesting and meaningful spoonerisms.

Placing spoonerisms too close to each other in a poem calls attention to the cleverness of your find. A better possibility for spoonerisms is to split them so their appearance in a poem provides a sense of unconscious unity, and is noticed only by the most careful readers. Indeed, some writers like to use imperfect spoonerisms or half-spoonerisms. In the following poem, notice the imperfect spoonerisms in "bound by worlds" and "blinded by words," and in "blood guess" and "God bless."

The Moon

lasted all night & seemed to burn
toward noon
after just that brief blue darkness
nightfall bound by worlds.

And we turn to that rising
again & again
we turn and like stars, like debutantes,
like false teeth
we come out.

How would we know
blinded by words

as we are

the blood guess of morning on the rocks
how it dawns on the gulls
creak of their throats against salt wind.

Here are some examples from Spooner himself, who was Dean
and Warden of New College at Oxford:

(In a sermon): Yes, Our Lord is indeed a shoving leopard.
(In another sermon): Which of us has not felt in his heart a
half-warmed fish?
(Proposing a toast): Let us drink to the queer old Dean.
(To a flunking student): Sir, you have tasted a whole worm.
You have hissed my mystery lectures. You were fighting a liar in
the quadrangle. You will leave Oxford by the town drain.

See also: WORD PLAY.

Stanza
("STAN-zuh")

The stanza is a group of lines in a poem separated from other lines by a space. *Stanza* is Italian for "room," and it might help to think of the relation of stanzas to a poem as rooms to a house. The stanza break (the space between stanzas) almost always indicates a pause, however slight, just as you have to slow down to go through a door. Other words for *stanza* are *verse* (as in "third verse, line 2") and *strophe*.

There are poems without stanza breaks, that you read from beginning to end and pause only where the punctuation indicates. It is possible to consider these poems as consisting of only one stanza, however long, but in such cases the stanza doesn't really figure.

Stanzas that don't follow a pattern are called "verse paragraphs."

Back when poems were set to music, the stanza conformed to the tune. To coincide with the musical line, the stanzas were of equal length and hewed closely in measure and beat. They followed strict patterns. As now, the song often had a stanza that served as refrain (a stanza that would be repeated at intervals throughout the song).

Even after poets no longer wrote for music, they continued to write poems that looked like those their predecessors set to music. Some poets didn't realize that the earlier poems had been written for music. And habit has its own force. But others just liked the way those songs looked. Since most people meet a poem first on the page, poets are very concerned with the way the poems look. For some poets, strict stanzaic patterns represent a challenge, for others the stanza is just an instruction to readers to pause. Some poets even use stanza breaks so the reader won't get confused or bored.

There are many traditional stanza forms. You can read other entries in this book to learn more about the many kinds of stanza you might want to try your hand at (quatrains, ottava rima, terza rima, ballads, etc.). The kind of stanza you select will not only depend on what you want to say, it will shape what you are able to say. Stanzaic forms have become vehicles for conveying certain experiences or emotions because over time it has become clear that they are most appropriate to their function, but it's always fun to try to write against the grain.

You can also invent your own stanza form. When some people build a house, they want every room to be the same size, because they think that size is ideal for rooms. Others will vary the size of each room according to how they expect it to be used, what they want to put in it, and who will stay there. The main thing is to make rooms that are big enough to be useful, shapely enough to be attractive, and not so empty as to be disappointing. Or you could write your poem first without stanza breaks and then go back and break the lines up into groups so that it all seems comfortable on the page.

Syllabic Verse
("sil-LAB-ic")

Syllabic verse is poetry with the same number of syllables in each line or with a regular pattern of numbers of syllables per line. *Normative syllabics* implies the same number of syllables in each line; *quantitative syllabics* establishes a syllabic pattern in the first stanza that is followed, line for line, in ensuing stanzas; *variable syllabics* establishes limits for the length of the lines, and works within those limits.

Writing in syllabics is a terrific way to "even out" a poem, and is useful also to writers who feel stymied when deciding where to break their lines. Syllabics are often introduced after the poem's first draft has been written: re-read each line, and, with each syllable, drum another finger on the table top to keep track. Write the number of syllables in each line at the beginning of that line, then review any patterns that may already exist or can be created with a minimum of tinkering.

Of course, no "rule" of poetic composition should be followed slavishly, and syllabics may be strictly or casually applied. Some writers insist on breaking the line wherever syllabics demand, while others refuse to hyphenate a word, and break their lines in only approximate accordance with a strict syllabic pattern. Writing in syllabics also creates the problem of determining how many syllables certain words have: is *scour* one or two syllables? Can *shower* be a one-syllable word? The use of a strict syllabic form can often influence how the reader pronounces such words. "Our turn is finally coming up" could be read as having eight or nine or ten syllables, depending on how many syllables are allowed for *our* and *finally*. Likewise, a word such as *history* can have two or three syllables, depending on the reader's oral interpretation; poets of the past sometimes would spell such a word "history" or "hist'ry" to tell the reader how many syllables to pronounce.

Souvenirs

and when the last war has been successful
when our history is sought by diggers
from another epoch, teeth will appear
in strata decades higher than our bones
as if we died on our backs
and sunk away from our mouths.

"Souvenirs" is a syllabic poem, with ten syllables (counting *history* in line two as a three-syllable word) in the first four lines, and seven syllables in each of the two final lines.

Certain poetic forms are based on syllabics. The cinquain consists of five lines, the first and fifth containing two syllables, and the second, third and fourth lines consisting of four, six and eight syllables, respectively. It is an American form. Another syllabic form, the haiku, consisting of three lines, the first and last five syllables each and the second seven syllables, originated in Japan.

The most famous syllabic verse poet is Marianne Moore (1887-1972). Read some of her poems, and read "The Picnic," a verse narrative by John Logan, available in poetry anthologies (such as *Contemporary American Poetry*, edited by Donald Hall) or in Logan's *Only the Dreamer Can Change the Dream: Selected Poems*. In "The Picnic" Logan uses lines of ten syllables each to tell the story of two teenagers who fall in love at a graduation outing. Use the poem as a model for your own narrative poem using a certain number of syllables per line. You might write about your own first "falling in love" experience, or someone else's. Or you might tell the story of a friendship — how it began and how it ended.

See also: CINQUAIN, HAIKU, SENRYU.

Tanka
("TON-ka")

Tanka (from the Japanese for "short poem") are mood pieces, usually about love, the shortness of life, the seasons, or sadness. Tanka use strong images and may employ the poetic devices, such as metaphor and personification, that haiku avoid.

The basic form of tanka is five lines, the first and third quite short and the second, fourth, and fifth a bit longer. Because the English language does not have the same kinds of rhythms as the Japanese, there is little point in counting syllables. Instead, following a pattern of accented syllables that goes line-by-line works well in English: two, three, two, three, three.

There are variations on the tanka form, the oldest dating back at least twelve hundred years. These early tanka presented one image or thought in the first two lines, then shifted to a related idea in the next three. (In the following example, "plovers" are small shore birds with a high-pitched cry.)

> thoughts of her
> unendurable, I go there . . .
> the winter night's
> river-wind is chill
> and plovers are crying
> — *Ki no Tsurayuki (ca.* A.D. *900),*
> *translated by William J. Higginson*

Written a thousand years later, the following tanka's speaking in plain words marks it as modern.

> "even now,
> shy, why notice only
> the springtime!"
> as I, eyes closed
> cling to his hand
> — *Yosano Akiko (1878-1942),*
> *translated by William J. Higginson*

Here is a tanka by a contemporary American poet:

Is the inlaid box
With a gilt hasp concealing
A letter, a jewel?
Within, a bunch of feathers,
The small bones of a bird.
— *Carolyn Kizer*

As with haiku, tanka can easily be ruined by too much sentimentality. To write some, try starting with images of real things in your own life that seem to match your mood. And try again another time, when your mood has changed.

See also: HAIKU, RENGA, SENRYU.

Tercet
("TUR-set" or "tur-SET")

The tercet (from the Latin word for *third*) is a stanza made of three lines, usually with rhyme. This form has a nice way of running the rhythm of the poem on in waves or bursts from stanza to stanza.

One of the most famous English poems that uses the tercet is "Ode to the West Wind" by Percy Shelley. The poet speaks to the wind in this, the poem's final section:

Make me thy lyre, even as the forest is:
What if my leaves are falling like its own!
The tumult of thy mighty harmonies

Will take from both a deep, autumnal tone,
Sweet though in sadness. Be thou, Spirit fierce,
My spirit! Be thou me, impetuous one!

Drive my dead thoughts over the universe
Like withered leaves to quicken a new birth!
And, by the incantation of this verse,

Scatter, as from an unextinguished hearth
Ashes and sparks, my words among mankind!
Be through my lips to unawakened earth

The trumpet of a prophecy! O, Wind,
If Winter comes, can Spring be far behind?

The modern poet William Carlos Williams has used the tercet form in many of his poems. He had always felt a need for an ordering principle in poetry at a time when the contemporary vogue had become "free verse." In this style, Williams thought, the rhythm of the poem had become so unattached from the words that the words had begun to drift around aimlessly. To bring the words back somewhat into the wave of energy carrying the poem, he began experimenting with three-line "stepped" groups, or tercets. He felt this form captured some of the phrasing he noticed in American speech. As he said,

> From the beginning I knew that the American language must shape the pattern. I noticed that I was particularly fascinated by [one] pattern: the dividing of the little paragraphs into lines of three.

This is his poem, "The Artist." (It has one word you might not know: *entrechat*. An entrechat is a ballet movement in which the dancer leaps into the air and repeatedly crisscrosses the feet so rapidly that they seem to blur.)

The Artist

Mr. T.
        bareheaded
                in a soiled undershirt
his hair standing out
        on all sides
                stood on his toes
heels together
        arms gracefully
                for the moment
curled above his head.
        Then he whirled about
                bounded
into the air
        and with an *entrechat*
                perfectly achieved
completed the figure.
        My mother
                taken by surprise
where she sat
        in her invalid's chair
                was left speechless.
Bravo! she cried at last
        and clapped her hands.
                The man's wife
came from the kitchen:
        What goes on here? she said.
                But the show was over.

When writing poems in this form, be attentive to the way your own ear "hears" the way words cluster together into groups or phrases, and "break" your lines at the appropriate pauses between these.

See also: LINE.

Terza rima
("TARE-tza REE-ma")

Terza rima is a tumbling, interlocking rhyme scheme which was invented by the thirteenth-century Italian poet Dante for the creation of his long poem, *The Divine Comedy*.

Terza rima (an Italian phrase meaning "third rhyme") consists of a series of three-line stanzas (tercets) with the rhyme scheme *aba, bcb, cdc, ded,* and so on. It can go on as long as the poet wishes. At the end of the poem an extra line is often added to complete the structure: *yzy z.*

It is thought that Dante invented the terza rima form to reflect the religious idea of the Trinity (*The Divine Comedy* is written in three books, each of which contains thirty-three [or thirty-three plus one] sections called cantos, and each section is written in tercets.).

Poets who have used terza rima in English and American poetry include: Robert Herrick, Chaucer, Thomas Wyatt, W.H. Auden, and Percy Bysshe Shelley, whose "Ode to the West Wind" begins:

> O wild West Wind, thou breath of Autumn's being,
> Thou, from whose unseen presence the leaves dead
> Are driven, like ghosts from an enchanter fleeing,
>
> Yellow, and black, and pale, and hectic red,
> Pestilence-stricken multitudes: O thou,
> Who chariotest to their dark wintry bed
>
> The wingèd seeds, where they lie cold and low,
> Each like a corpse within its grave, until
> Thine azure sister of the Spring shall blow
>
> Her clarion o'er the dreaming earth, and fill
> (Driving sweet buds like flocks to feed in air)
> With living hues and odours plain and hill:
>
> Wild Spirit, which art moving everywhere;
> Destroyer and preserver; hear, oh, hear!

Shelley chose to vary the rhyme scheme by ending each section of the poem with a rhymed couplet (two-line stanza), so it goes: *aba, bcb, cdc, ded, ee.*

If you like rhyming, try terza rima. The beauty of it is that it creates a link between one stanza and another so that people will want to keep reading the poem with excitement and they will remember it. The hard part is finding enough good and surprising rhymes in American English that don't seem strained or corny. But remember that you can take liberties when rhyming, as in the popular singer Tom Waits's lyric: "wasted and wounded / it ain't what the moon did. . . ."

See also: TERCET, OTTAVA RIMA, STANZA.

Triolet

The word *triolet* is pretty, like a flower, resembling the word *violet* in looks, but pronounced "TREE-o-LAY." The "tri" (meaning "three") refers to the fact that the opening line occurs three times in this form. The triolet is an eight-line poem with two rhymes and two repeating lines. The first line is repeated as the fourth and seventh lines, and the second and eighth lines are the same.

If we make a diagram with the two rhymes designated as A and B respectively, and let A^1 stand for the first repeated line and B^2 the second repeated line, it would look like this:

A^1
B^2
A
A^1
A
B
A^1
B^2

A French form, the triolet can be traced back to the thirteenth century as the simplest form of the rondel (a poem of twelve or fourteen lines). In fact, it appears that the triolet, the rondel, and the rondeau are a single genre with variations.

The triolet was cultivated especially by French medieval poets such as Jean Froissart and Eustace Deschamps, but fell into disuse during the end of the fifteenth and during the sixteenth centuries. It was revived by Jean de la Fontaine (the writer of fables) in the seventeenth, and continued to be used through the nineteenth century.

With several exceptions, there were few triolets written in English until recent times, and it still has not become a widely practiced form.

Here is an anonymous triolet from the thirteenth century, in both the original French and an approximate translation.

Encore un chapelet ai	A^1
Qui fut m'amie;	B^2
Donnés me fut de cuer gai.	A
Encore un chapelet ai;	A^1
Pour s'amour le garderai	A
Toute ma vie;	B
Encore un chapelet ai	A^1
Qui fut m'amie.	B^2

I still have a bouquet	A^1
That belonged to my love	B^2
It was given to me with a heart so gay	A
I still have the bouquet	A^1
For her sake I will keep it this way	A
As long as I live;	B
I still have the bouquet	A^1
That belonged to my love.	B^2

The words *love* and *live,* rather than being perfect rhymes, are near-rhymes. Although most traditional triolets celebrated love and were cheerful and playful in tone, this contemporary triolet has a different quality, as well as variations in the repeated lines:

Triolet

A perfectly clear liquid like water flows out of the spine
Last night in the hospital this is what I saw
I don't know where this fluid sits & what its design
A perfectly clear liquid like water flows from her spine
Does it move from her brain in a line?
The cool doctor draws it out with a straw
A perfectly clear liquid like water flows out of the spine
Last night, in the cold hospital, this is what I saw.

The poet wrote this poem after visiting her mother in the hospital.

The triolet is a relatively easy form to work with because of its short length and repeating lines. The two opening lines determine the poem's flavor and feel. You might want to begin by simply writing down two lines that you would say to a friend in conversation; or you might think of a subject, such as your street, and write two statements (not necessarily connected to one another) concerning that street. After writing the two opening lines, you could then repeat the opening lines further down where they belong, and then jump into the poem from there.

See also: RONDEAU.

Villanelle
("villa-NELL")

The words *villain* and *villanelle* come from the Latin (or Italian) word *villa,* which means "country house" or "farm." Originally a villain wasn't a bad character in a story, he was simply a farm servant, a country bumpkin. The *villanella* was an old Italian folk song with an accompanying dance. Since the seventeenth century, the villanelle has had its current form, although it has moved, in the hands of contemporary poets, to themes other than love or the joys of country living.

A French poet, Jean Passerat (1534-1602), wrote a poem in the late 1500s which he entitled "Villanelle," and the form of this poem came to be the strict form for all villanelles.

In the villanelle there are six stanzas; the first five stanzas are three lines long and the final stanza is four lines long. The first line and last line of the first stanza take turns repeating as the final line of the next four stanzas, and then are rejoined as the last two lines of the poem. The poem has a rhyme scheme of *a, b, a* throughout, except in the last stanza where there is a slight variation.

The structure isn't as complicated as it sounds. Take this first villanelle by Passerat:

Villanelle

I have lost my dove:	A^1
Is there nothing I can do?	*b*
I want to go after my love.	A^2
Do you miss the one you love?	*a*
Alas! I really do:	*b*
I have lost my dove.	A^1
If your love you prove	*a*
Then my faith is true;	*b*
I want to go after my love.	A^2

Haven't you cried enough?	*a*
I will never be through:	*b*
I have lost my dove.	*A*¹
When I can't see her above	*a*
Nothing else seems to do:	*b*
I want to go after my love.	*A*²
Death, I've called long enough,	*a*
Take what is given to you:	*b*
I have lost my dove,	*A*¹
I want to go after my love.	*A*²

The letters at the end of each line stand for the rhyme scheme. All the *a*'s rhyme and so do all the *b*'s. A^1 is the first line of the poem and A^2 is the last line of the first stanza. Sometimes when either of these two lines reappear, they take on a new meaning.

There's something soothing or hypnotic about the sound of a villanelle, the way the lines come back, like waves at the ends of the stanzas. The form also carries a tone of conviction that reinforces its sentiments.

In the nineteenth century, another French writer, Leconte de Lisle, used the form of the villanelle but wrote more serious, philosophical poems. Continuing in this vein, the American poet Edwin Arlington Robinson wrote a somber villanelle ("House on the Hill") just after the turn of the century. About a house that has been left empty, it is written in short, simple sentences. "They are all gone away, / The house is shut and still, / There is nothing more to say." In 1935, Dylan Thomas wrote "Do Not Go Gentle into That Good Night." This very serious villanelle is about not giving in to death and it is written eloquently, with long, dramatic lines.

Do Not Go Gentle Into That Good Night

Do not go gentle into that good night,
Old age should burn and rave at close of day;
Rage, rage against the dying of the light.

Though wise men at their end know dark is right,
Because their words had forked no lightning they
Do not go gentle into that good night.

Good men, the last wave by, crying how bright
Their frail deeds might have danced in a green bay,
Rage, rage against the dying of the light.

Wild men who caught and sang the sun in flight,
And learn, too late, they grieved it on its way,
Do not go gentle into that good night.

Grave men, near death, who see with blinding sight
Blind eyes could blaze like meteors and be gay,
Rage, rage against the dying of the light.

And you, my father, there on the sad height,
Curse, bless, me now with your fierce tears, I pray.
Do not go gentle into that good night.
Rage, rage against the dying of the light.

Another notable villanelle is Theodore Roethke's "The Waking."

The Waking

I wake to sleep, and take my waking slow.
I feel my fate in what I cannot fear.
I learn by going where I have to go.

We think by feeling. What is there to know?
I hear my being dance from ear to ear.
I wake to sleep, and take my waking slow.

Of those so close beside me, which are you?
God bless the Ground! I shall walk softly there,
And learn by going where I have to go.

Light takes the Tree; but who can tell us how?
The lowly worm climbs up a winding stair;
I wake to sleep, and take my waking slow.

Great Nature has another thing to do
To you and me; so take the lively air,
And, lovely, learn by going where to go.

This shaking keeps me steady. I should know.
What falls away is always. And is near.
I wake to sleep, and take my waking slow.
I learn by going where I have to go.

It is possible to write all different sorts of poems using the basic, fairly complex structure of the villanelle. Think of something you feel strongly about. Then write two lines that are approximately the same length and that rhyme. These two can be your repeating lines, in other words lines A^1 and A^2. Once you have those two lines and you are happy with what they say, then let your head and heart dance around with the other lines of the poems. Writing a villanelle is like working a jigsaw puzzle; you can move the lines around quite a bit until they finally seem to fit, to make a kind of poetic sense.

Word Play

A sense of word play is common to all good poets. It's not that their works are always playful, but that they show a delight in the language, an awareness of its history and its feel, and a pleasure in what makes it sound good in relation to what it means.

There are many ways that words can play: through their rhythm, rhyme, alliteration, assonance, puns, spoonerisms, surprise, and others. Poems that do little *but* play can be interesting, witty, and even hypnotic, as in:

> I saw Esau sawing wood,
> And Esau saw I saw him;
> Though Esau saw I saw him saw
> Still Esau went on sawing.

Such playful poems don't have the weight of poems that combine play with substance. On the other hand, poems that have a "serious" message and little else are boring and dead.

When poems have a nice play of words in them, it is as if the words are dancing, either dramatically and wildly or simply and slowly: the sounds and appearances of the words—their weights and tones and colors—are dancing, the same way the meaning is dancing among the words, all moving together in patterns that are right for that poem.

Appendix A: Other Forms

Some poetic forms and techniques in this book are not listed under their own headings. They are discussed under other headings. The list below is a guide to these passing references.

Amoebean poetry: see PASTORAL POEM.
Caesura: see LINE.
Dada poem: see PERFORMANCE POEM.
Enjambment: see LINE.
Feminine rhyme: see RHYME.
Futurist poem: see CALLIGRAM.
Kenning: see METAPHOR.
Light rhyme: see RHYME.
Masculine rhyme: see RHYME.
Measure: see RHYTHM, LINE.
Mistranslation: see IMITATION.
Mock epic: see EPIC.
Normative syllabics: see SYLLABIC VERSE.
Octave: see SONNET.
Pastourelle: see PASTORAL POEM.
Protest poem: see OCCASIONAL POEM.
Quantitative syllabics: see SYLLABIC VERSE.
Sestet: see SONNET.
Simile: see METAPHOR.
Slant rhyme: see RHYME.
Strophe: see STANZA.
Variable syllabics: see SYLLABIC VERSE.
Verse paragraph: see STANZA.

Appendix B: Authors Cited

In the following list, the abbreviation *ca.* stands for *circa,* the Latin word for "around." For example, "ca. 1763" means "around 1763." The abbreviation *b.* stands for *born.* A question mark indicates there's some uncertainty about the exact year. Some authors are quoted in the text but not listed below because the text makes it clear who they are.

Apollinaire, Guillaume (1880-1918). French poet.
Apuleius, Lucius (second century A.D.). Roman satirist, philosopher.
Archilochos (probably seventh century B.C.). Greek poet.
Ariosto, Ludovico (1474-1533). Italian poet.
Aristophanes (448?-380 B.C.?). Greek comic dramatist.
Aristotle (384-322 B.C.). Greek philosopher.
Ashbery, John (b. 1927). American poet.
Auden, W.H. (1907-73). American (English-born) poet.
Baker, Russell (b. 1925). American journalist.
de Banville, Théodore (1823-91). French poet.
Baraka, Amiri (b. 1934). American poet.
Basho, Matsuo (1644-94). Japanese poet.
Baudelaire, Charles (1821-67). French poet.
Beerbohm, Max (1872-1956). English critic, caricaturist.
Benchley, Robert (1889-1945). American humorist.
Benét, Stephen Vincent (1898-1943). American poet, fiction writer.
Berrigan, Ted (1935-83). American poet.
Bertrand, Aloysius (1807-41). French poet.
Blue Cloud, Peter (b. 1933). American poet.
Bly, Robert (b. 1926). American poet.
Boccaccio, Giovanni (1313-75). Italian writer.
Browning, Elizabeth Barrett (1806-61). English poet.
Browning, Robert (1812-89). English poet.
Byron, Lord (George Gordon) (1788-1824). English poet.
Buchwald, Art (b. 1925). American journalist.
Calverly, C.S. (1831-84). British parodist.
de Campos, Haroldo (b. 1929). Brazilian poet, translator.
Cangiullo, Francesco (1888-1977). Italian poet-painter.
Carroll, Lewis (1832-98). English mathematician, author.
Cavalcanti, Guido (1255-1300). Italian poet.
Cernuda, Luis (1904-63). Spanish poet.
Chaucer, Geoffrey (1340?-1400). English poet.
Coleridge, Samuel Taylor (1772-1834). English poet.
Collom, Jack (b. 1931). American poet.
Cortazar, Julio (1914-84). Argentinian fiction writer.

Cortez, Jayne (b. 1936). American poet.
Creeley, Robert (b. 1926). American poet.
Cummings, E.E. (1894-1962). American poet.
Dahlberg, Edward (1900-77). American fiction writer.
Daniel, Arnaut (ca. 1150-ca. 1200). French troubador poet.
Dante (Dante Alighieri) (1265-1321). Italian poet.
De La Mare, Walter (1873-1956). English poet, novelist.
Deschamps, Eustace (ca. 1346-ca. 1406). French poet.
Dobson, Austin (1840-1921). English poet, biographer, essayist.
Donne, John (ca. 1572-1631). English poet.
Dryden, John (1631-1700). English poet, dramatist.
Dulot (ca. 1600-ca. 1650). French poet.
Dumas, Alexandre (1824-95). French novelist, dramatist.
Dybeck, Stuart (b. 1942). American writer.
Dylan, Bob (b. 1941). American songwriter, singer.
Edson, Russell (b. 1935). American poet.
Eliot, T.S. (1888-1965). British (American-born) poet, critic.
Ellison, Ralph (b. 1914). American novelist, essayist.
Emerson, Ralph Waldo (1803-82). American essayist, poet.
Fielding, Henry (1707-54). English novelist.
Finlay, Ian Hamilton (b. 1925). Scottish poet, toymaker, sculptor, typographer.
Follain, Jean (1903-71). French poet.
Froissart, Jean (1333?-1400?). French historian.
Frost, Robert (1874-1963). American poet.
Fuller, Buckminster (1895-1983). American engineer, architect, writer.
Gautier, Théophile (1811-72). French poet, critic.
Ginsberg, Allen (b. 1926). American poet.
Goeritz, Matthias (b. 1915). Mexican (German-born) poet.
Goethe, Johann Wolfgang von (1749-1832). German poet, dramatist.
Gosse, Sir Edmund (1849-1928). English poet, critic.
Gray, Thomas (1716-71). English poet.
Guthrie, Woody (1912-67). American songwriter, singer.
Hafiz (fourteenth century). Persian poet.
Hall, Donald (b. 1928). American poet, essayist.
Hardy, Thomas (1840-1928). English novelist, poet.
Harjo, Joy (b. 1951). American poet.
Harte, Bret (1836-1902). American writer.
Hawthorne, Nathaniel (1804-64). American author.
H.D. (Hilda Doolittle) (1886-1961). American poet.
Hegemon of Thasos (fifth century B.C.). Greek poet, satirist.
Herbert, George (1593-1633). English poet.
Herrick, Robert (1591-1674). English poet.
Homer (850 B.C. or earlier). Greek epic poet.
Hopkins, Gerard Manley (1844-89). English poet.
Horace (65-8 B.C.). Roman poet.
Huelsenbeck, Richard (1892?-1974). German poet.
Hugo, Victor (1802-85). French poet, novelist, dramatist.
Hulme, T.E. (1883-1917). English critic, philosopher, poet.

Ibsen, Henrik (1828-1906). Norwegian dramatist.
Ignatow, David (b. 1914). American poet.
Jami (1414-92). Persian poet.
Jonson, Ben (1573?-1637). English poet, dramatist.
Joyce, James (1882-1941). Irish fiction writer, poet.
Juvenal (60?-140). Roman poet, satirist.
Kharms, Daniel (1905-42). Russian poet.
Koch, Kenneth (b. 1925). American poet.
Labé, Louise (ca. 1524-ca. 1565). French poet.
la Fontaine, Jean de (1621-95). French poet, author of fables.
Lattimore, Richmond (1906-84). American poet, translator.
Lear, Edward (1812-88). English painter, nonsense poet.
da Lentino, Giacomo (ca. 1200-1250). Italian poet.
Lindsay, Vachel (1879-1931). American poet.
Leconte de Lisle (1818-84). French poet.
Logan, John (b. 1923). American poet.
Lorca, Federico Garcia (1896-1936). Spanish poet, dramatist.
Lowell, Amy (1874-1925). American poet.
Lowell, Robert (1917-77). American poet.
Lucian (second century A.D.) Greek satirist.
Lucilius (180-102 B.C.). Roman satirist.
Machaut, Guillaume de (1300-77). French poet, composer.
Mallarmé, Stéphane (1842-98). French poet.
Marot, Clément (1496-1544). French poet.
Martial (ca. 40-ca. 102). Roman epigrammatist.
Marvell, Andrew (1621-78). English poet.
Matthews, James Brander (1852-1929). American educator, author.
Melville, Herman (1819-91). American novelist.
Merwin, W.S. (b. 1927). American poet, translator.
Michaux, Henri (1899-1985). French poet, painter.
Millay, Edna St. Vincent (1892-1950). American poet.
Milton, John (1608-74). English poet.
Mimnermus of Colophon (seventh century B.C.). Greek poet.
Molière (Jean Baptiste Poquelin) (1622-73). French dramatist.
Moore, Marianne (1887-1972). American poet.
Morgan, Edwin (b. 1920). Scottish poet.
Morgenstern, Christian (1871-1914). German poet.
Nash, Ogden (1902-70). American poet.
Norton, Thomas (1532-84). English poet, lawyer.
Ochs, Phil (1940-76). American songwriter, singer.
Odassi, Tisi degli (Michele de Bartolomeo Odassi) (ca. 1450-ca. 1492).
    Italian poet.
O'Hara, Frank (1926-66). American poet.
Olson, Charles (1910-71). American poet.
d'Orléans, Charles (1391-1465). French poet.
Ortiz, Simon (b. 1941). American poet.
Ovid (43 B.C.?-17 A.D.). Roman poet.

Perelman, S.J. (1904-79). American writer.
Perse, St.-Jean (1887-1975). French poet, diplomat.
Petrarch (Francesco Petrarca) (1304-74). Italian poet.
Petronius, Gaius (first century A.D.). Roman satirist.
Pindar (522?-443 B.C.). Greek poet.
de Pisan, Christine (1363?-1431). French (Italian-born) author of
     allegories.
Plath, Sylvia (1932-63). American poet.
Plautus (254?-184 B.C.). Roman dramatist.
Ponge, Francis (b. 1899). French poet.
Pope, Alexander (1688-1744). English poet.
Porter, Cole (1893-1964). American songwriter.
Pound, Ezra (1885-1972). American poet, translator, critic.
Propertius, Sextus (50?-15 B.C.?). Roman poet.
Rabelais, François (1494?-1553). French satirist.
Reverdy, Pierre (1889-1960). French poet.
Reznikoff, Charles (1894-1976). American poet.
Richardson, Samuel (1689-1761). English novelist.
Rilke, Rainer Maria (1875-1926). Czech poet, novelist, wrote in
     German and French.
Rimbaud, Arthur (1854-91). French poet.
Robinson, Edwin Arlington (1869-1935). American poet.
Roethke, Theodore (1908-63). American poet.
Ronsard, Pierre de (1524-85). French poet.
Rothenberg, Jerome (b. 1931). American poet.
Rumi (Jalal ud-din Rumi) (1207-73). Persian poet.
Sackville, Thomas (1536-1608). English poet, diplomat.
Sappho (ca. 600 B.C.) Greek poet.
Sanai. Persian poet.
Schiller, Johann Christoph Friedrich von (1759-1805). German poet,
     dramatist.
Schwerner, Armand (b. 1927). American poet.
Shakespeare, William (1564-1616). English poet, dramatist.
Shelley, Percy (1792-1822). English poet.
Sidney, Sir Philip (1554-86). English poet, statesman.
Siefert, Louisa (nineteenth century). French poet.
Skelton, John (1460?-1529). English poet.
Smith, Stevie (1902-71). English poet.
Sophocles (496?-406 B.C.). Greek dramatist.
Spenser, Edmund (1552?-99). English poet.
Stein, Gertrude (1874-1946). American writer.
Stephen, J.K. (1859-92). British writer.
Stevens, Wallace (1879-1955). American poet.
Swift, Jonathan (1667-1745). English (Irish-born) satirist.
Tate, Allen (1899-1979). American critic, poet.
Tennyson, Alfred, Lord (1809-92). English poet.
Theocritus (third century B.C.). Greek poet.
Thomas, Dylan (1914-53). Welsh poet.

Thoreau, Henry David (1817-62). American writer, philosopher.
Thurber, James (1894-1961). American humorist.
Tibullus, Albius (54?-18? B.C.). Roman poet.
Twain, Mark (Samuel Clemens) (1835-1910). American humorist.
Tzara, Tristan (1896-1963). French (Rumanian-born) poet.
Ungaretti, Giuseppe (1888-1970). Italian poet.
Virgil (70-19 B.C.). Roman poet.
Wakoski, Diane (b. 1937). American poet.
Waldman, Anne (b. 1945). American poet.
White, E.B. (1899-1985). American writer.
Whitman, Walt (1819-92). American poet.
Williams, Emmett (b. 1925). American poet, visual artist.
Williams, William Carlos (1883-1963). American poet, fiction writer.
Wordsworth, William (1770-1850). English poet.
Wright, James (1927-80). American poet.
Wyatt, Sir Thomas (1503?-42). English poet, diplomat.

Bibliography

In addition to the books listed by category below, there are many useful reference books to consult to learn more about poetic forms. Among them are *The Princeton Encyclopedia of Poetry and Poetics* edited by Alex Preminger (Princeton, N.J.: Princeton University Press, 1974); *The Longman Dictionary and Handbook of Poetry* edited by Jack Myers and Michael Simms (New York: Longman, 1985); *Poetry Handbook* by Babette Deutsch (New York: Barnes & Noble Books, 1974); *The Oxford English Dictionary;* and the *Encyclopaedia Britannica* (the eleventh edition, if you can find it; otherwise, any edition).

Abstract Poem

Sitwell, Edith. *The Collected Poems* (New York: Vanguard Press, 1954).

Alphabet Poem

Abish, Walter. *Alphabetical Africa* (New York: New Directions, 1974). A novel.

Ballad

Child, Francis James. *The English and Scottish Popular Ballads* (New York: Dover Books, 1965).

(An excellent collection of recordings of folk ballads is that of the Folk Recordings Archive, Recorded Sound Division, Library of Congress, Washington, D.C. 20540. Catalog available on request.)

Ballade

Villon, François. *The Poems of François Villon,* translated by Galway Kinnell (Hanover: University Press of New England, 1982).

Blues

Handy, W.C., editor. *Blues: an Anthology, Complete Words and Music of 53 Great Songs* (New York: Collier Books, 1971).

Neff, Robert and Connor, Anthony. *Blues* (Boston: David R. Godine, Publisher, 1975).

Calligram

Apollinaire, Guillaume. *Calligrammes,* translated by Anne Hyde Greet (Berkeley: University of California Press, 1980).

Themerson, Stefan. *Apollinaire's Lyrical Ideograms* (London: Gaberbocchus Press, 1968).

Chant

Rothenberg, Jerome, editor. *Technicians of the Sacred* (Garden City, N.Y.: Doubleday & Co., 1968; Berkeley: University of California Press, 1986).

————. *Shaking the Pumpkin* (Garden City, N.Y.: Doubleday & Co., 1972).

Trask, Willard, editor. *The Unwritten Song: Poetry of the Primitive and Traditional Peoples of the World* (New York: Macmillan, 1966).

Collaboration

Koch, Kenneth, editor. *Locus Solus: Special Collaborations Issue,* No. 2 (Lans-en-Vercors, France, 1961).

Concrete Poem

Williams, Emmett, editor. *An Anthology of Concrete Poetry* (New York: Something Else Press, 1967).

Couplet

Pope, Alexander. *The Poems of Alexander Pope,* edited by Maynard Mack (New Haven: Yale University Press, 1969).

————. *Poems of Alexander Pope* (Baltimore: Penguin, 1953).

Eclogue

Virgil. *The Pastoral Poems,* translated by E.V. Rieu (Baltimore: Penguin, 1967).

Elegy

Bailey, John C. *English Elegies* (London & New York: John Lane, 1900; reprinted by Arden Library).

Rilke, Rainer Maria. *The Duino Elegies,* translated by J.B. Leishman and Stephen Spender (New York: W.W. Norton, 1939).

Epigram

Jay, Peter, editor. *The Greek Anthology* (New York: Oxford University Press, 1973).

Epitaph

Kippax, J.R. *Churchyard Literature: a Choice Collection of American Epitaphs* (Chicago: S.C. Griggs & Co., 1877).

Loaring, H.J. *Epitaphs: Quaint, Curious, and Elegant* (London: W. Tegg, 1873).

Event Poem

Kirby, Michael. *Happenings* (New York: E.P. Dutton, 1965).

Kaprow, Allan. *Assemblages, Environments & Happenings* (New York: Harry N. Abrams, Inc., 1965).

Foot

Fussell, Paul. *Poetic Meter and Poetic Form* (New York: Random House, 1979).

Found Poem

Reznikoff, Charles. *Testimony* (New York: New Directions, 1965).

Ghazal

Ghalib. *Ghazals of Ghalib,* translated by Aijaz Ahmad and others (New York: Columbia University Press, 1971).

Haiku

Blyth, R.H., editor. *Haiku* (Tokyo: Hokuseido Press, 1949-52). Four volumes.

———— Blyth, R.H. *A History of Haiku* (Tokyo: Hokuseido Press, 1963-64).

Heuvel, Cor van den, editor. *The Haiku Anthology: Haiku and Senryu in English* (New York: Simon & Schuster, 1986).

Higginson, William J. *The Haiku Handbook: How to Write, Share, and Teach Haiku* (New York: McGraw-Hill, 1985).

Imitation

Lowell, Robert. *Imitations* (New York: Farrar, Straus and Cudahy, 1961.)

Insult Poem

Lewis, Richard, editor. *Out of the Earth I Sang* (New York: W.W. Norton, 1968).

Trask, Willard, editor. *Classic Black African Poems* (New York: Eakins Press, 1968).

Light Verse

Auden, W.H., editor, *The Oxford Book of Light Verse* (London: Oxford University Press, 1941).

Armour, Richard. *Writing Light Verse and Prose Humor* (Boston: The Writer, 1971).

List Poem

Berrigan, Ted. *So Going Around Cities* (Berkeley: Blue Wind, 1980).

Ginsberg, Allen. *Collected Poems* (New York: Harper & Row, 1984).

Whitman, Walt. *Leaves of Grass* (New York: Random House, The Modern Library, no date).

Lune

Collom, Jack. *Moving Windows: Evaluating the Poetry Children Write* (New York: Teachers & Writers Collaborative, 1985).

Kelly, Robert. *Lunes* (New York: Hawk's Well Press, 1964). Bound into one volume with Jerome Rothenberg's *Sightings*.

Macaronic Verse

Wells, Carolyn, editor. *A Nonsense Anthology* (New York: Dover Books, 1958).

Lewis, D.B. Wyndham and Lee, Charles, editors. *The Stuffed Owl* (New York: Capricorn, 1962).

Nonsense Verse

Grigson, Geoffrey, editor. *The Faber Book of Nonsense Verse* (Faber & Faber: London and Boston, 1979).

Wells, Carolyn, editor. *A Nonsense Anthology* (New York: Dover Books, 1958).

Ode

Neruda, Pablo and Vallejo, Cesar. *Selected Poems*, translated by Robert Bly and others (Boston: Beacon Press, 1971).

Parody

MacDonald, Dwight. *Parodies: An Anthology from Chaucer to Beerbohm — and After* (New York: Random House, 1960).

Pastoral

Barrell, John and Bull, John. *The Penguin Book of Pastoral Verse* (New York: Penguin, 1982).

Virgil. *The Pastoral Poems,* translated by E.V. Rieu (Baltimore: Penguin, 1967).

Performance Poem

Vincent, Steve and Zweig, Ellen, editors. *The Poetry Reading* (San Francisco: Momo's Press, 1981).

Projective Verse

Olson, Charles. "Projective Verse" in *The New American Poetry: 1945-1960* (New York: Grove Press, 1960), edited by Donald Allen.

Prose Poem

Benedikt, Michael. *The Prose Poem: An International Anthology* (New York: Dell, 1976).

Jacob, Max. *The Dice Cup* (New York: SUN, 1979).

Rap

Hager, Steven. *Hip Hop* (New York: St. Martin's Press, 1984).

Toop, David. *The Rap Attack* (London: Pluto Press, 1984).

Renga

Kondo, Tadashi and others. *Twelve Tokyo Renga* (Fanwood, N.J.: From Here Press, 1987).

Mayhew, Lewis, translator. *Monkey's Raincoat: Linked Poetry of the Basho School with Haiku Selections* (Tokyo: Charles E. Tuttle Press, 1985).

Sato, Hiroaki. *One Hundred Frogs: From Renga to Haiku to English* (New York: Weatherhill, 1983).

Ritual Poem

(See books listed under **Chant.**)

Senryu

Blyth, R.H. *Senryu: Japanese Satirical Verses* (Tokyo: Hokuseido Press, 1949).

————. *Japanese Life and Character in Senryu* (Tokyo: Hokuseido Press, 1960).

(See also listings under **Haiku.**)

Sestina

Action Poétique, No. 99 (Avon, France, 1985). Special issue on the sestina. Mostly in French.

Sonnet

Barnes, Richard. *Episodes in Five Poetic Traditions* (San Francisco: Chandler-Intext, 1972)

Bender, Robert M. and Squier, Charles L. *The Sonnet: A Comprehensive Anthology* (New York: Washington Square Press, 1965)

Withers, Carl. *The Penguin Book of the Sonnet* (Baltimore: Penguin, 1944).

Tanka

Goldstein, Sanford. *Gaijin Aesthetics* (La Crosse, Wisc.: Juniper Press, 1983).

Miner, Earl. *An Introduction to Japanese Court Poetry* (Stanford, Calif.: Stanford University Press, 1968).

Sesar, Carl. *Takuboku: Poems to Eat* (Tokyo: Kodansha, 1966).

Word Play

Borgmann, Dmitri A. *Language on Vacation* (New York: Scribner's, 1965).

Davis, Harold Thayer. *The Fine Art of Punning* (Evanston: Principia Press of Illinois, 1954).

Espy, Willard R. *An Almanac of Words at Play* (New York: C.N. Potter, 1975).

————. *The Game of Words* (New York: Bramhall House, 1972).

Farb, Peter. *Word Play: What Happens When People Talk* (New York: Knopf, 1974).

Huizinga, Johan. *Homo Ludens: A Study of the Play Element in Culture* (Boston: Beacon Press, 1955).

OTHER T&W PUBLICATIONS YOU MIGHT ENJOY

Poetic Forms. Ten 30-minute audio programs on ten basic poetic forms. "Informal, lively, and appealing.... Highly useful to teachers and to anyone who would like to try writing poetry"—*Choice*.

The List Poem: A Guide to Teaching & Writing Catalog Verse by Larry Fagin defines list poetry, traces its history, gives advice on teaching it, offers specific writing ideas, and presents more than 200 examples by children and adults.

Pantoum. A computer writing game based on the poetic form. 5 ¼" floppy disk for use on any Apple II series computer. "*Pantoum* sparks the imagination and stimulates interesting, original, new connections between words and ideas"—*The Writing Notebook*.

Acrostic. As above. "Makes writing acrostic-style poems a game.... Useful for vocabulary and whole-language programs"—*Booklist*.

The T&W Guide to Walt Whitman, edited by Ron Padgett. Fifteen poets offer practical ideas for fresh ways to read Whitman and to write poetry and prose inspired by him. "A lively, fun, illuminating book"—Ed Folsom, University of Iowa, editor of *The Walt Whitman Quarterly Review*.

The Poetry Connection: An Anthology of Contemporary Poems with Ideas to Stimulate Children's Writing by Nina Nyhart and Kinereth Gensler. "An entirely indispensable classroom tool"—*California Poets-in-the-Schools*.

Moving Windows by Jack Collom. An in-depth guide to evaluating the poetry children write. "A landmark book . . . stimulating ideas that any teacher could utilize and wonderful examples of children's poems"—*Oregon English*. "First rate"—*Rolling Stock*. "Superb"—*Fessenden Review*.

The Writing Workshop, Vols. 1 & 2 by Alan Ziegler. A perfect combination of theory, practice, and specific assignments. "Invaluable to the writing teacher"—*Contemporary Education*.

The Whole Word Catalogue, Vols. 1 & 2. T&W's best-selling guides to teaching imaginative writing. "*WWC 1* is probably the best practical guide for teachers who really want to stimulate their students to write"—*Learning*. "*WWC 2* is excellent.... It makes available approaches to the teaching of writing not found in other programs"—*Language Arts*.

•

For a complete catalogue of T&W books, magazines, audiotapes, videotapes, and computer writing games, contact Teachers & Writers Collaborative, 5 Union Square West, New York, NY 10003–3306, tel. (212) 691-6590.